P9-DDS-234

ALSO BY PAT AND GINA NEELY

Down Home with the Neelys

THE NEELYS' CELEBRATION
COOKBOOK

THE NEELYS' CELEBRATION
COOKBOOK

DOWN-HOME MEALS FOR EVERY OCCASION

Pat Neely and Gina Neely

with **ANN VOLKWEIN**

photographs by **BEN FINK**

ALFRED A. KNOPF   NEW YORK   2011

THIS IS A BORZOI BOOK
PUBLISHED BY ALFRED A. KNOPF

Copyright © 2011 by Patrick Neely and Gina Neely
Photographs copyright © 2011 by Ben Fink
Illustrations copyright © 2011 by Robert W. Shepperson

All rights reserved. Published in the United States by Alfred A. Knopf,
a division of Random House, Inc., New York, and in Canada
by Random House of Canada Limited, Toronto.

www.aaknopf.com

Knopf, Borzoi Books, and the colophon
are registered trademarks of Random House, Inc.

A portion of this work was originally published in
Food Network magazine (November 2011).

Library of Congress Cataloging-in-Publication Data
Neely, Patrick.
The Neelys' celebration cookbook : down-home meals for every occasion /
Pat Neely, Gina Neely, with Ann Volkwein ; photographs by Ben Fink.
p.   cm.
ISBN 978-0-307-59294-1 (hardback)
1. Entertaining. 2. Holiday cooking. I. Neely, Gina. II. Volkwein, Ann.
III. Title. IV. Title: Celebration cookbook.
TX731.N44 2011
642'.4—dc23   2011030268

Jacket photograph by Ben Fink
Jacket design by Barbara de Wilde
Manufactured in the United States of America

First Edition

GINA *This book is dedicated to a higher power, as it could not have been accomplished without His hand in it, as well as to all who share a love of entertaining and bringing people together for the pure enjoyment of food and the celebratory communion of souls. Oink.*

PAT *GOD has truly blessed me all the years of my life with many celebrations. My mom, Lorine, celebrated traditional holidays and everything in between in our fun, loving, Christian home. And today my soul mate, Gina, shares and carries on these traditions beautifully, no matter how busy we are in our lives. Our hope is that our daughters Shelbi and Spenser will carry this on when they begin their own families.*

And we hope this book will bring you all joy and happiness when you plan your next family gathering.

To God, my family, my wife, and my two adorable daughters, I say, "Raise your glasses and let's get the party started!"

CHEERS!

Contents

September

October

November

December

 If you see this little guy, it means this recipe takes more than one hour to prepare. So plan ahead!

THE NEELYS'
CELEBRATION
COOKBOOK

Introduction

We hope you enjoyed getting to know our family and cooking some of our favorite recipes in our first book, but now . . . it's party time! With a little Pat-and-Gina magic, we'd like to show you how to "Neely-tize" a holiday or special occasion to create a memorable event for everyone to enjoy. This book serves up new ways to celebrate the holidays, as well as introducing some holidays of our own. Gina can't stand those long stretches between the "real" holidays, so she pulls together romantic Mini-Moons, turns it up for Movie Nights, and throws Girls' Nights to be remembered. Think outside that box when you entertain!

Everybody teases Gina for throwing parties for any small reason or occasion, but shouldn't life be celebrated every chance you get? It's about sharing joy and loving the here and now. As we all know, cooking is a lot like therapy: food has a way of breaking the ice and helping you start fresh, so you can get relationships right (even on the fifth try, if need be), and entertaining is an excuse to bring all kinds of folks together. Throwing a party is like brewing a special potion of togetherness, and thank God it works!

So get ready to cook up some great dishes with a big shot of love, because, at the end of the day, you can't enjoy the meal without an open heart.

Let's get the party started. . . . Whoo-hoo!

Throwing a Party, Gina-Style

PAT So often we're told that if a man truly admires his mother he'll look to marry a woman with some of her same distinct qualities. Well, I admit it: Gina and Mom can be like night and day, yet they both love to entertain at home and have family around. It's odd, because I didn't see that right away with Gina: she was so good-looking, and the good-looking girls I'd previously dated were so focused on strutting their stuff that they couldn't even boil water! But once I realized that I'd found "the whole package" in Gina, it was a happy surprise.

GINA Pat's mom hosted the first Christmas Eve dinner we celebrated as a married couple. Now, Pat's mom and I really are very similar in our hosting styles, but she likes to do things over-the-top *all the time*. Don't get me wrong, I believe that there is a time and place for all of that. But I've got a little "old school" in me as well! Everything at that Christmas dinner was so pretty, and the table was beautiful: the desserts were exquisite, and there were elaborate turkeys, hams, and dressings.

So I was checking the table out, and all of a sudden I realized something was missing. I asked, "Where are the corn bread and cranberry sauce?" Pat's mom replied, "We don't eat cranberry sauce; we eat glazed apples." I almost laid myself out on that floor! I had to do something quickly, so I said, "Oh, I forgot something. I'll be right back," and headed straight to the corner store for a cornbread mix and a can of cranberry sauce. (Forget my homemade cranberry relish, on page 249; this was an emergency!) And now here we are, fifteen years later, and Pat and I have hosted every single Thanksgiving and Christmas since that first time. Our house has become holiday headquarters, and Mama Neely doesn't mind a bit! Nowadays she can walk in with one of her Mama Neely specialties, help us finish up the cooking, then have a glass of wine and cross her legs. After all, she's been hosting these holidays for more than twenty-five years for her six children—she's earned a break!

PAT In many ways, this book could be titled "How to Party like Gina," because she's truly a master of hosting events and putting on the good times. Watching her decorate, plan a menu, and assemble a guest list is kind of like watching a kid get ready for Christmas. You're gonna hear about every detail for weeks and months building up to the event. Some of this may have to do with the role Gina used to have as the head of catering at Neely's: she can wrangle together a party for ten to ten thousand people and get all the details just right, from utensils to uniforms, the whole nine yards. She "brings it" when she's entertaining at home, too.

And, oh my God, she is raising two more holiday-event coordinators in Spenser and Shelbi. So you can imagine what it must be like to walk in my shoes, with three women in the house, when it's Movie Night and they're getting all excited about which movies, where we're sitting, which great dishes we're going to nibble on while watching. . . . I used to complain about all the work that went into even the most minor event, but I love my family, and I can have a blast with just the four of them—which of course includes Zoe, our two-year-old Shih Tzu!

Pat's Top Ten Party Tips for Guys

To me, throwing a party is kind of like getting ready for a trip. You've got to pack and prepare your house to go away, which may feel overwhelming, but once you get to the vacation site, it's paradise. It's been that way for years in our house. I don't think Gina knows how to do a subtle celebration (in my opinion, just like my mom!), and she's not indecisive—she knows what she wants. So, in light of my years of experience helping Gina, I've got some tips for the guys out there like me.

1 If Mama ain't happy, ain't nobody happy.

2 Hands off the guest list. In our household, I have input on about 10 percent of the list! (And that's fine with me. Gina rules the party anyway, and always invites people I enjoy.)

3 Be prepared to do *all* of the "Honey Do"s. ("Honey, do this. . . . Honey, get the box out of the car. . . . Honey, get the grocery list. . . .")

4 Inform all your golf buddies to give you a rain check. Forget it, no golf.

5 Put your weightlifting belt on. There's going to be some heavy lifting.

6 The best reply: "Yes, dear" (and with a smile!). Guys, it's much easier to say yes than no, and what follows when you say yes is so much better.

7 Restock your bar, because you may need a drink before the guests arrive.

8 Designate a personal corner. Every time we have a big family gathering, I find myself a peaceful corner after the party is really going, so I can just observe, and sometimes—most of the time—it is a true joy to admire the loved ones around me. Seize that moment. (I also do a head count, so I can tell Gina how many folks she really invited, or how many showed up. Two Thanksgivings ago, I counted fifty-seven people: I've got five siblings, Gina has four, there were mothers, cousins, nieces, and nephews, and then the third of the group that was unrelated but whom we still call family. I have toyed with the idea of installing a turnstile just so I don't have to keep counting.)

9 Try to avoid segregating the women and the men. Gina hates it when the guys are watching a game upstairs, so she'll come up and remind them to get downstairs and mingle (Super Bowl and March Madness being the exceptions to this rule).

10 Start to clean up before the party is over. If you start picking up and taking the trash out, you'll usually find that two or three people will pitch in, and then the others will feel guilty and ask how they can help.

Gina's Top Ten Holiday Tips

I know the holidays tend to be overwhelming, so I'll let you in on some tips that work for me. The thing to always keep first and foremost in your mind is to *have a good time*—even if that means buying some prepared dishes, or designating a bartender if you're worried about time or not feelin' the hoopla. As a woman who wears a lot of hats, I say it's okay for us to cheat every now and then. . . . Sometimes it's not cheating, it's being smart!

1 First, we want to give ourselves a good *woosa*. That's a deep breath: in through the nose, and out through the mouth. It's how we relax, relate, and release.

2 Recognize that you're human and everything may not go as planned. When something doesn't work out, just laugh!

3 Determine how large the party will be; will it be an intimate or a large gathering?

4 Do you want to do everything yourself, or throw a potluck? (Sometimes I find the downside to a potluck comes around if everyone arrives promptly, or if people start dropping off loads of stuff the day before. Try to prevent both! If you opt to do everything yourself, take the next step to heart.)

5 The key to the menu is preparation, preparation, preparation. If there's anything that you can do ahead of time, *do it*. Do all the chopping and prepping you can, and determine which dishes can be made and stored in the fridge, waiting to be warmed up the day of the big event. (Sometimes I start several days before!)

6 For the bar, I usually suggest a house signature cocktail instead of a variety of drinks, plus a nonalcoholic offering of some sort. Fill up a colorful cocktail tray, and bring the drinks to greet your guests at the door. You'll find that people love trying something new and festive, and not having to stock a full bar is easier on your wallet in the long run.

7 If you have a theme to your menu, you may want to think about translating that to the decor, but don't get too crazy. You can get into color schemes, but

New Year's Eve Dinner with Friends

GINA When Pat and I first got together, every intimate celebratory moment was precious, so the very first New Year's Eve was just for us. Since we didn't have much money, we had some appetizers and a decent bottle of champagne. Later, we'd occasionally go to a big party, and we have great memories of trips to New Orleans, but New Year's really got Neely-tized when our girls got involved—and it only takes the four of us to get a party started. A lot of years, Pat would be working hard and long at the restaurant, but he'd bring home sausage and wings, and barbecue nachos, and we'd all tune in to Dick Clark and watch the ball drop—the girls toasting with sparkling cider, us toasting with champagne.

Now the girls are older, so New Year's Eve is a time of reflection and anticipation of the year ahead for us all. We'll invite a few couples over with their children; my sister Tanya will come, as well as some of the girls' friends. It's very relaxed: not a party with a lot of hoopla, horns, and confetti, but with good stories, soft music, and games like Taboo or charades. (Now, that means multi-generational teams—Pat says he gets teased for not understanding the board games too well and screwing up the rules, but in the long run we have a lot of fun!)

KICKIN' OFF THE YEAR WITH TEENS

In a few years, our girls will be out at big parties for New Year's, so we take advantage of our time now to show them that New Year's doesn't have to be about putting on fancy clothes and going out on the town. (Huge parties mean a lot of strangers, kissing your spouse, dancing a little, and trying to get home by 1 or 2 a.m.!) But remember: to celebrate with teenagers, you have to include them in the planning process, from whom they want to invite to what's on the menu. So serve dishes they like, pull out the board games, and team up—you'll sleep a lot better if the kids are at home, and they'll have a lot of fun as well. We hope the girls continue the tradition, so one day we'll be celebrating with our grandchildren!

New Orleans BBQ Shrimp

On New Year's Eve 1996, we decided we wanted a warmer place to celebrate, so we jumped on a train to New Orleans, took a paddleboat down the Mississippi, and ate dinner while watching the fireworks. The next day, there was the Sugar Bowl game and the Court of Two Sisters on Royal Street, in the French Quarter, where we went for mimosas and brunch. This routine became a tradition for a few years—but now it doesn't beat toasting in the year with our girls, so we brought the flavors home. This recipe holds a particularly funny memory for us. One year we had a bowl of some of these saucy, spicy shrimp at a restaurant on the pier, just before jumping on the paddleboat. Pat couldn't keep the spoon away from his mouth, and he ended up spilling a tremendous amount of that dark roux down the front of his white sweater. So there he was, sipping champagne and watching the fireworks with a huge stain! He didn't mind a bit. **MAKES 6 APPETIZER SERVINGS**

2 pounds large shrimp, peeled and deveined

2 tablespoons Cajun seasoning

2 tablespoons canola oil

6 cloves garlic, smashed and peeled

One 12-ounce light-bodied beer

Juice of 1 lemon

One 8-ounce bottle clam juice

¼ cup hot sauce, preferably Tabasco

¼ cup Worcestershire sauce

2 tablespoons apple-cider vinegar

2 dried bay leaves

1 teaspoon whole black peppercorns

½ cup (1 stick) cold butter, cut into cubes

1 crusty French baguette

Toss the shrimp with the Cajun seasoning in a medium bowl. Set aside.

Heat the canola oil in a large saucepan over medium-high heat. Once it's hot, toss in the garlic, and sauté until golden, about 3 or 4 minutes. Add the shrimp to the pan, and cook until they turn bright pink, about 1 minute more. Remove the shrimp from the pan with a slotted spoon, and set aside on a plate. Pour in the beer, lemon juice, clam juice, hot sauce, Worcestershire sauce, apple-cider vinegar, bay leaves, and peppercorns; bring to a simmer, and cook for 15 minutes, until the liquid is slightly thickened.

Whisk the cubes of butter into the sauce, and once it's melted, add the shrimp to finish cooking, about 2 minutes more. Serve the shrimp and sauce in bowls with loads of crusty bread for dipping.

Pat's Deep-Fried Cornish Game Hens

I love Cornish hens: baked or smoked, but also deep-fried. To me they're like smaller turkeys, so they're perfect for entertaining smaller groups or just your family. If you can't find them at your butcher counter, check the frozen-meat section—just be sure to let them thaw out completely. Because of their small size, you can use an electric fryer instead of the larger turkey contraptions for deep-frying them (another bonus). Deep-fried, they've got a golden crust and a juicy, juicy tenderness. If you're short on fridge space, divide the marinade between two or three large zip-top bags, and divide the Cornish hens among them. Press the air out and seal tight; then you can fit them into a smaller space. Now, Shelbi and Gina might share a hen, so for light eaters just split one bird down the middle. But a heavy eater like me will eat a whole hen. I've been anticipating it all day! **SERVES 6 OR MORE**

1 tablespoon kosher salt

1 tablespoon crushed red-pepper flakes

1 tablespoon freshly ground black pepper

1 tablespoon poultry seasoning

2 teaspoons cayenne pepper

2 teaspoons lemon-pepper seasoning

3 quarts buttermilk

1 onion, cut into wedges

1 bunch fresh thyme sprigs

Six 1½-pound Cornish game hens

Peanut oil, for frying

2 cups all-purpose flour

Whisk together the first six ingredients in a small bowl. Set half of this mixture aside.

Divide the remaining seasoning mixture between two large mixing bowls, and pour the buttermilk evenly between the two bowls, whisking to combine. Put half of the onion and thyme in each bowl. Place three game hens in each mixing bowl, and turn to coat. Cover the bowls with plastic wrap, and leave in the fridge for 8 hours or overnight (the longer the better; allow the seasonings and flavors to permeate the game hens).

Heat the peanut oil to 375 degrees F in a large Dutch oven or deep-fryer. (For tips on deep-frying, see page 19.) Preheat your oven to 200 degrees F, and cover two heavy-duty sheet trays with wire racks. Remove the game hens from the buttermilk mixture while the oil is heating.

Whisk together the flour and the remaining seasoning mixture in a large casserole. Working with one game hen at a time, put one game hen in the flour and toss to coat, then shake off the excess. Slip the coated game hens, in batches according to the size of your fryer, into the hot oil, and fry for 13 minutes, until beautifully golden brown. Place each fried hen on the wire-rack-fitted sheet tray, and hold in the warm oven. Repeat with remaining hens.

ALTERNATIVE

Baked Cornish Game Hens

Heat the oven to 400 degrees F. Cover two heavy-duty rimmed sheet trays with wire racks, and spray with nonstick spray.

Drain the hens from the buttermilk marinade, and pat dry. Place the hens on the sheet trays, drizzle with olive oil, and season with salt and pepper.

Put the pan in the oven, and roast for 45 minutes, or until an instant-read thermometer inserted into the thickest part of the thigh registers 165 degrees F and the juices run clear.

Pat's Guide to Deep-Frying

One of the things I think people really don't know about me is that I was frying food before I was grilling! (Nowadays my love of fried food comes second only to my love of grilling.) Fried food in the South is like pizza in Chicago: if you grew up in Memphis, you grew up with it. My grandfather used to fry whole rabbits, and my grandmother used to fry chicken for breakfast, served up with biscuits!

1 CHOOSE YOUR OIL   Neutral oils like peanut, safflower, canola, and vegetable oil all have a high "smoke point," so they work well at high frying temperatures. We often like to use peanut oil, because it adds a very subtle peanut flavor; the flavor of canola oil is less pronounced.

2 PICK YOUR POT   If you don't have an electric fryer, select a heavy-bottomed Dutch oven for deep-frying. You'll usually need at least 3 or 4 inches of oil in the bottom of the pan, but more if you're frying something larger, like Cornish game hens or chicken.

3 FILL IT UP   Be careful not to overfill your pot! If you don't leave room for the items you're frying, the oil may spill over the sides, causing a mess or, even worse, a fire. To check how much oil you need, you can first do a test run with water. Fill the pot up with water, then slip in the food you're going to fry. Wherever the water rises to, that's how high your oil is going to go—so mark that place on the pot, and don't fill it too high!

4 HEAT IT UP If the temperature of your oil is too low, you'll be left with a greasy, pale crust minus that great crunch we all love. If it's too high, you'll have a dark brown, burnt crust that's undercooked on the inside. It's always best to use a deep-fry thermometer for accurate cooking, but if you don't have one, test the temperature by slipping into the oil a little corner or edge of the food you're planning to fry. If the oil is at the right temperature, it will bubble up and sizzle around the food.

5 SLIP IT IN Using caution, gently slip the food into the oil, so you don't splatter and burn yourself. Don't plop it in!

6 DON'T OVERCROWD Adding too much to your fryer at once will lower the oil temperature, resulting in soggy, pale food instead of the crispy, golden-brown crust you're going for. So fry in batches for best results.

7 TAKE THE FOOD'S TEMPERATURE Be sure to have a meat thermometer handy when cooking poultry of any kind. (I've been served fried chicken that looked beautiful on the outside but was raw on the inside.) Insert the thermometer into the thickest part of the breast or thigh, and make sure it comes to around 160 degrees F before you pull it from the oil. Onion rings, potato chips, and French fries are easier to gauge by sight; with something like hush puppies, it's best to break the food open and test for doneness.

8 DRAIN AND SALT Remove the food with tongs or a spider sieve, and let the food drain on a paper-towel-lined plate or sheet tray to remove the excess oil. Season while the food is still hot. (You want the salt to stick to the oil!)

Dirty-Rice Collard Green Bundles

PAT You won't find a collard green—or a green of any kind, for that matter—that Gina hasn't mastered and found a dozen ways to cook. She's queen of the twists on greens. The idea for this particular twist came from stuffed cabbage with a vinegary red sauce—but we think this is even better than that recipe. Don't you? **SERVES 6 TO 8**

SAUCE

1 large onion, finely chopped

3 cloves garlic, finely chopped

2 tablespoons canola oil

One 28-ounce can plain tomato sauce

¼ cup light brown sugar

¼ cup apple-cider vinegar

Kosher salt and freshly ground black pepper

1 large bunch collard greens (about 18 leaves), stalks discarded

DIRTY-RICE FILLING

1 tablespoon canola oil

½ pound sweet Italian pork sausage, removed from casing

1 large onion, finely chopped

1 medium green bell pepper, seeded and finely chopped

2 stalks celery, finely chopped

2 cloves garlic, minced

1 cup chicken broth

¼ teaspoon cayenne pepper

2 cups cooked long-grain white rice

¼ cup chopped fresh parsley leaves

Kosher salt and freshly ground black pepper

Preheat the oven to 350 degrees F.

To start the sauce: Sauté the onion and garlic in the oil in a heavy-bottomed saucepan set over medium-high heat, until softened, about 3 minutes. Stir in the tomato sauce, brown sugar, apple-cider vinegar, salt, and pepper. Bring to a boil, then reduce the heat, and let simmer for 15 minutes, so all the flavors can build.

Set a large pot of water to boil. Lay each collard leaf out on your work surface, and remove the tough large stem and center vein. Don't cut the whole leaf in half; just cut out the toughest part of the stem in a V-shape. Once the water is boiling, slip the collard leaves in and cook until tender, about 15 minutes. Drain into a colander, and rinse with cold water to help stop the cooking.

While the sauce is simmering, begin the dirty-rice filling: Heat the oil in a heavy-bottomed sauté pan set over medium-high heat. Brown the sausage, breaking it up with a wooden spoon. Once the sausage is browned, add the onion, green bell pepper, celery, and garlic, cooking until softened, about 5 minutes more. Stir in the chicken broth, cayenne, cooked rice, and parsley, mixing thoroughly and letting the broth reduce until there is no moisture left in the pan. Taste, and season with salt and pepper.

Lay out each cooked collard leaf and put ¼ cup of the dirty rice in the center. Fold both the sides into the center, and the top and bottom over the center. Roll up into a cylinder—tightly, like a cigar or a small burrito. If there happen to be any remaining leaves, you can chop them up and add to the sauce.

Pour a ½-inch layer of the sauce into a 13-by-9-inch casserole dish. Arrange the collard rolls, seam sides down, on top of the sauce. Pour the remaining sauce over the stuffed collards, and cover the pan with foil. Bake in the preheated oven for 40 minutes. Remove from the oven, and serve.

Bourbon Bread Pudding

Here we go back to New Orleans again, with Bourbon Street flair. Southern bourbon-soaked brioche bread makes a hearty Creole-style dessert. **SERVES 10**

2 tablespoons butter, plus more for greasing

10 cups cubed brioche bread (from a 1-pound loaf)

1 cup chopped pecans

4 cups half-and-half

1 cup whole milk

5 eggs, beaten

1 cup packed dark-brown sugar

3 tablespoons bourbon

2 teaspoons pure vanilla extract

1 teaspoon ground cinnamon

½ teaspoon kosher salt

¼ teaspoon grated nutmeg

Butter a 13-by-9-inch baking dish, and put the cubed brioche in it. Sprinkle with the pecans.

Whisk together the half-and-half, milk, eggs, butter, brown sugar, bourbon, vanilla, cinnamon, salt, and nutmeg in a large bowl.

Pour the custard mixture over the bread in the baking dish, giving the bread a stir to make sure it's coated. Let the pudding sit for 1 hour, so the bread can fully absorb the milk.

Preheat the oven to 350 degrees F. Once it is ready, put the dish in the oven and bake for 50 minutes, or until puffy and set. Remove, and let stand 10 minutes before serving. This is absolutely lovely when served with some fresh whipped cream.

Gina's Hoppin' John Soup

GINA Ever since I was a little girl, my mom has been telling me that if you don't eat black-eyed peas on New Year's Day you'll have a bad year ahead of you. Now, when I was younger I didn't care a bit. I was going through that awkward stage anyway—how much worse could it be?

But as I got older, I learned to love that black-eyed pea tradition, convinced that my year was going to be fantastic! And you know what's funny? I tell my girls the same thing. Who says traditions and superstitions aren't effective? Not to mention that black-eyed peas are rich in calcium and vitamin A. What could be bad about that? Of course, this being a Gina recipe, I added in my favorite collard greens. . . . Mmm, even better. **SERVES 4 TO 6**

1 small bunch (about 1 pound) collard greens

2 tablespoons olive oil

6 ounces smoked ham steak, cut into ¼-inch cubes

1 medium onion, chopped

4 cloves garlic, minced

1 medium carrot, chopped

1 stalk celery, chopped

¼ teaspoon crushed red-pepper flakes

Kosher salt and freshly ground black pepper

6 cups low-sodium chicken broth

1 dried bay leaf

One 15½-ounce can black-eyed peas, drained and rinsed

One 15-ounce can diced tomatoes, with juices

1 cup cooked long-grain white rice

Dash of hot sauce, preferably Tabasco

Dash of Worcestershire sauce

Parmesan cheese, grated, for topping

Remove the stems and center ribs from the collard greens. Stack about six leaves on top of each other, roll into a cigar shape, and slice into thin ribbons.

Heat the olive oil in a large, heavy pot over medium-high heat. When the oil is hot, toss in the ham, onion, garlic, carrot, and celery, and cook, stirring, until the vegetables are tender, roughly 4 minutes. Sprinkle in the red-pepper flakes, and season with salt and pepper. Add the collard greens, and sauté until they begin to soften.

Pour in the chicken broth, the bay leaf, the black-eyed peas, and the can of tomatoes with their juices. Bring to a simmer, and cook for 30 minutes. Stir the rice into the soup to warm. Taste for seasoning, and add more salt and pepper, hot sauce, and Worcestershire sauce.

Spoon into bowls, and sprinkle each bowl with Parmesan cheese.

Super Bowl Sunday

GINA As we all know, Super Bowl is generally a time for the boys to get together, but the new trend is that a lot of women are joining the club. I hear more women discussing sports as eagerly as men, which I love, because this is just another way for all of us to communicate as couples.

Pat and I love a good debate, but the Super Bowl or its menu is not one that we disagree on. Unfortunately, you can't count me in as a member of the "new club," because "Super Shopping" is still my choice, not Super Bowl. But the great thing about the Super Bowl is . . . I am not even missed! As you can imagine, in Pat's house, with five football-playing boys, Super Bowl Sunday was always a big deal. As he tells it . . .

PAT'S BROTHERS IN FOOTBALL

PAT I grew up as one of five boys. Our father was born with sickle-cell disease, always small and spending a lot of time going to the doctor, so he was never able to play sports growing up. I think that's why he introduced us all to football at a very young age, and was adamant that we play sports. I can remember back when my brother Tony was no more than in grade school: my father bought him an Atlanta Falcons uniform, complete with helmet and shoulder pads—the whole nine yards!

I started playing in my Catholic-school parochial league in probably first or second grade. We always wanted to please our father, and he didn't miss a game. During Saturday Little League and right after Sunday mass, we'd head out to the field, and if you scored a touchdown or a play, you knew you'd be in Daddy's good graces for a whole week. It felt like being on cloud nine. To my sorrow, my father passed away when I was in sixth grade, but he would've been proud of me, because by middle school I'd evolved into a decent athlete, just like my brothers, and I felt him cheering me on in spirit.

Gaelin, my oldest brother, was the front-runner. In junior high and high school, he wore the number 40 . . . so all the younger brothers looking up to him from our respective grades and schools also had to wear 40. He chose the number 40 because it was Gale Sayers' number: Gale was a top Hall of Fame running back for the Chicago Bears, and we'd all watched the movie *Brian's Song,* about Brian

Piccolo, who died of cancer while still playing for the Bears. Gale was his best friend, and we idolized him. Football was something that kept all of my brothers close, and it keeps us close even now.

Nowadays all of us Neely brothers get together for the Super Bowl, and we include Gina's brother Ronnie in the big day. We're never all rooting for the same team, and that just adds more excitement. (I can tell my brothers Mark and Gaelin, "I told you so!" when my team scores!) Gina will come around and flip the channel to *Sex and the City,* giving us the business—we always need to have that spice on Super Bowl Sunday. But we always end up back on the game, yelling and cheering and having a good time.

And then there's always the question "What are we eating?" As the years went on and we opened the restaurants, we just had to have something connect us to our roots! Having pulled pork on skins gave us a bit of both our loves: classic football, and great barbecue. This type of menu gives you the feeling of being at a bar with a bunch of guys, with great flavorful appetizers to nibble on during the game, and a spicy beer. (And there's nothing sweeter than a chocolate peanut-butter brownie to cool the palate.)

Country-Fried Jalapeño Poppers

PAT Gina's told me before, "If you like the kickoff, then you're going to love these poppers!" They have the perfect amount of kick to them. Between the smokiness of the paprika and the heat of the cayenne pepper, take one bite and the game is on!

We remove the jalapeño seeds so that the poppers aren't too hot, but leave them in if you like really spicy. After all, I am a hot man, and I mean that both palate-wise and physical-wise (and, as you can tell, I'm very, very humble). Jalapeños are a vegetable that you can get seriously creative with: filling them up with cheese, using buttermilk in a batter, and deep-frying these little puppies makes one of the best appetizers you can imagine. **SERVES 4**

Peanut oil, for frying

16 medium jalapeño peppers

2 tablespoons butter

1 small shallot, minced

4 cloves garlic, minced

Kosher salt and freshly ground
  black pepper

1 cup grated pepper-Jack cheese

4 ounces cream cheese, softened

2 cups self-rising flour

2 tablespoons smoked paprika

½ teaspoon cayenne pepper

1 cup buttermilk

1 egg, beaten

Preheat your oil in a Dutch oven or fryer to 375 degrees F. (For tips on deep-frying, see page 19.)

Make a long slit from the stem of each jalapeño to the bottom. Make another slit across the top of the pepper, creating a T-shape. Remove the seeds and ribs with a small paring knife, or, if you prefer it fiery hot, leave the seeds and ribs intact.

Melt the butter in a small sauté pan over medium-high heat. Once it foams, add the shallot and garlic, and sauté until tender. Season with salt and pepper. Scrape the shallot and garlic into a bowl, and let cool.

Once the shallot and garlic are cool, stir in the pepper Jack and the cream cheese. Carefully stuff the jalapeños with the cheese mixture, and push the seams closed to seal (the cheese mixture inside will stick and hold them shut).

Whisk together the flour, smoked paprika, cayenne, and a pinch of salt and pepper in a large bowl. Whisk together the buttermilk and the egg in a separate, small bowl. Dredge the stuffed peppers through the flour, then the buttermilk, and then the flour again. If you like, take a second run through the buttermilk and another dip in the flour, so you have some extra crunch in your popper.

Working in batches, gently place the jalapeños in the hot oil in the fryer and fry until golden brown, about 2 minutes. Drain on a paper-towel-lined platter, and season with salt and pepper.

Let cool for just a few minutes before serving. These suckers will be hot!

Pat's Sweet and Spicy Grilled Wings with Smoky Blue Cheese Dipping Sauce

PAT I absolutely love making my grilled hot wings. Gina calls me the grill master: I'm a grill king *and* a wingman. There is nothing better than wings with a smoky grilled flavor mingling with a sweet, spicy, and creamy dipping sauce.

One of the best things about living in Memphis is that we can grill year-round, even on a 35-degree day (which is the normal temperature on Super Bowl Sunday). Grilling wings can be completed in a 10-minute period outside, so even if it's chilly out, you can stand it! **SERVES 6**

WINGS

3 pounds chicken wings, cut at the joint, washed, and dried well

¼ cup canola oil

2 tablespoons lemon-pepper seasoning

1 tablespoon kosher salt

1 teaspoon chipotle chile powder

4 tablespoons unsalted butter

2 tablespoons Dijon mustard

2 tablespoons honey

¼ cup hot sauce, preferably Tabasco

1 tablespoon apple-cider vinegar

1 teaspoon chipotle chile powder

Dash of Worcestershire sauce

Kosher salt and freshly ground black pepper

2 tablespoons sliced green onions, for garnish (optional)

1 scant cup smoky blue cheese dipping sauce (recipe follows)

Toss the chicken wings with the oil, and sprinkle with lemon-pepper seasoning, salt, and chile powder in a large bowl. Cover with plastic wrap, and leave the bowl in the fridge for 30 minutes, letting the flavors marry together while you prepare the grill.

Heat your grill to medium-high direct heat, using charcoal. Once it's hot, grill the wings for 7 to 9 minutes per side, until crisp and completely cooked through.

Combine the butter, mustard, honey, hot sauce, vinegar, chile powder, Worcestershire, salt, and pepper in a large saucepan set over medium heat. Taste for seasoning, and add more chipotle if you want it spicier. Allow the sauce to come to a simmer.

Once the sauce is simmering, cut the heat and add the wings, and toss thoroughly in the sauce. Remove to a large platter, sprinkle with green onion, and serve with the smoky blue cheese dipping sauce.

SMOKY BLUE CHEESE DIPPING SAUCE

MAKES 1 SCANT CUP

¼ cup crumbled Danish blue cheese

¼ cup buttermilk

¼ cup sour cream

2 teaspoons apple-cider vinegar

1 teaspoon smoked paprika

2 tablespoons thinly sliced green
onions

Kosher salt and freshly ground
black pepper

Mash the blue cheese with a fork into the buttermilk and sour cream in a small bowl, thoroughly breaking it up. Pour in the vinegar, paprika, and green onion and mix well. Season with salt and pepper, cover with plastic wrap, and let rest in the fridge for at least 30 minutes, so the flavors can marry.

Gina's "Double Pig" Grilled Potato Skins

GINA For some reason, there are always potatoes in the pantry. So pull them out and make some potato skins! Grilling them gives them a nice spin, and since we are the first family of barbecue, these skins are complemented by barbecue sauce, pulled pork, and bacon. And you guys all know how I feel about the pig... so I like to call these the "double pig."

They also make a nice pick-me-up when you're entertaining, so, to make them more like appetizers, you can slice them in quarters, arrange on a platter, and sprinkle with green onions. Trust me, these will be eaten so fast they'll be history.

PAT That's right, pig layered on pig, y'all! Having potato skins, and adding two types of pork—bacon and pulled pork—truly puts a guy (that's me, Pat!) in hog heaven. For you non–pig lovers (surely only a few of you), you can always substitute turkey bacon, chicken, or even beef brisket for the bacon and pulled pork. **SERVES 6**

4 large russet potatoes, scrubbed

¼ cup (½ stick) butter

2 cloves garlic, minced

¼ teaspoon cayenne pepper

Kosher salt and freshly ground black pepper

1 cup shredded cheddar cheese

½ cup Neely's BBQ sauce (see page 37), warmed

½ pound BBQ pork (see pages 163 or 164)

Sour cream, for topping

4 slices bacon, cooked, crumbled

Green onions, sliced, for garnish

Preheat the oven to 350 degrees F.

Pierce the potatoes with a fork, and spread on a baking sheet. Place on the middle rack of the oven, and bake until fork-tender, about 1 hour. Remove from oven, and let sit until the potatoes are cool enough to handle.

Preheat the grill to medium heat.

Cut the potatoes in half lengthwise, and spoon out the flesh, leaving a ½-inch shell of meat on the skin.

Melt the butter in a saucepan, then toss in the minced garlic and cayenne pepper. Liberally brush the potato insides with the butter mixture, then flip each over and butter the skin. Sprinkle the skin with salt and freshly ground black pepper.

Place the potatoes, skin side up, on grill, and cook until crisp, about 4 or 5 minutes, then flip and grill an additional 4 or 5 minutes on other side.

Remove from the grill to a platter. Pile the cheese, barbecue sauce, and pulled pork into the hot potatoes. Top with the sour cream, crumbled bacon, and green onions for garnish.

BBQ Chili Mac

This dish reminds us of warmth and comfort, and it also adds heartiness to the menu. Being served BBQ chili mac basically means a big "welcome to the Neely home."

Cavatappi are great noodles for this dish, because they're shaped like corkscrews, so you can grab all the good stuff and get the full flavor. If you can't find cavatappi, elbow macaroni comes in a distant second. **SERVES 8 TO 10**

Kosher salt and freshly ground black pepper

1 pound cavatappi pasta

1 tablespoon olive oil

4 slices bacon, diced

1 large onion, chopped

2 jalapeño peppers, ribs and seeds removed, chopped

4 cloves garlic, chopped

1½ pounds lean ground beef

3 tablespoons tomato paste

1 cup Neely's BBQ sauce (recipe follows)

One 14-ounce can crushed tomatoes

One 28-ounce can diced tomatoes in juice

One 15-ounce can ranch-style pinto beans

Dash of hot sauce, preferably Tabasco

Green onions, sliced, for garnish

Sour cream, for garnish

Grated cheddar cheese, for garnish

Bring a large pot of salted water to a boil. Once it's boiling, add the pasta and cook until it's al dente. Drain well in a colander, toss in olive oil, and reserve.

Cook the bacon in a large Dutch oven over medium heat until it is just lightly crisp and its fat has rendered. Toss in the onion, jalapeño, and garlic, and sauté until tender. Add the beef to the veggies to brown, breaking up with a wooden spoon. Plop the tomato paste into the pan, and stir until incorporated. Stir in the BBQ sauce, crushed tomatoes, diced tomatoes, and beans, and simmer for 20 minutes, to allow the flavors to marry. Taste for seasoning, and add hot sauce and salt and pepper if desired. Add the pasta to the meat mixture, and stir well to combine.

Serve in bowls, garnished with green onions, sour cream, and cheddar cheese.

NEELY'S BBQ SAUCE

MAKES 3½ CUPS

2 cups ketchup

1 cup water

½ cup apple-cider vinegar

5 tablespoons light-brown sugar

5 tablespoons granulated white sugar

½ tablespoon freshly ground black pepper

½ tablespoon onion powder

½ tablespoon ground mustard

1 tablespoon lemon juice

1 tablespoon Worcestershire sauce

In a medium saucepan, combine all ingredients. Bring mixture to a boil, and reduce heat to simmer. Cook, uncovered, stirring frequently, for 1 hour 15 minutes.

Chocolate and Peanut Butter Brownie Bites

GINA Can you imagine life without these two amazing ingredients? Who would want that? It would be like having fabulous shoes without a great handbag. Having chocolate and peanut butter is heaven on earth. If you think I talk a lot, give me chocolate and peanut butter and you won't hear another word out of me!

MAKES 36 SMALL BROWNIES

BATTER

¾ cup (1½ sticks) unsalted butter

2 cups semisweet chocolate chips, divided

½ cup all-purpose flour

½ teaspoon baking powder

¼ teaspoon table salt

⅓ cup packed light-brown sugar

½ cup granulated white sugar

2 large eggs

2 large egg yolks

1 teaspoon pure vanilla extract

PEANUT BUTTER SWIRL ("GET YO SWIRL ON!")

2 tablespoons unsalted butter, at room temperature

¼ cup confectioners' sugar

¾ cup smooth peanut butter

1 teaspoon pure vanilla extract

Pinch of table salt

Preheat the oven to 350 degrees F. Adjust a rack to the center of the oven.

Line an 8-by-8-inch baking pan with parchment or foil, leaving a 2-inch overhang over the edges. Cover the pan with some nonstick cooking spray.

Melt the butter and 1 cup chocolate chips together in a heavy-bottomed saucepan set over medium heat, stirring constantly. Remove from heat and cool slightly.

Whisk together the flour, baking powder, and salt in a medium bowl. Set aside.

Once the chocolate is slightly cool, stir the brown sugar, granulated sugar, eggs, egg yolks, and vanilla into the saucepan until smooth. Stir the flour mixture into the saucepan until thoroughly combined. Pour in the remaining cup of chocolate chips.

To make the peanut butter filling: Beat together the butter, confectioners' sugar, peanut butter, vanilla, and salt in a medium bowl until smooth.

Pour the chocolate batter into the prepared pan. Spoon large dollops of the peanut butter mixture evenly across the top of the batter. Use the tip of a knife or a toothpick to make pretty swirls with the peanut butter throughout the chocolate.

Bake for 40 minutes, or until a toothpick inserted into the center comes out clean. Remove from the oven, and let cool completely on a wire rack before cutting into squares.

Michelada Beer Cocktails

GINA Pat says no Super Bowl should ever be viewed without a beer, but I'm the queen of cocktails, and who needs regular beer when you can have a Michelada cocktail? When we filmed the show *Road Tasted with the Neelys,* we discovered this spicy beer in Santa Fe, where it is generally served during Fiesta. It has such a unique flavor, and sometimes it's nice to mix it up and serve the totally unexpected . . . but you definitely need to be ready for the spice.

If you want to add a little something special, you can rim your glasses with lime, put salt and chile powder on a separate plate, and dip the rims of the glasses in it—just to give the cocktail a little something extra!

Go ahead—drink it, and score a touchdown! **MAKES 2 COCKTAILS**

3 tablespoons kosher salt

2 teaspoons chile powder (optional)

1 lime, wedged, for garnish

¼ cup Rose's Lime Juice

Two 12-ounce Mexican beers, preferably Corona

2 dashes of hot sauce, preferably Tabasco (yes, this is the kick!)

Place the salt (mixed with chile powder, if using) in a small dish. Rub a lime wedge over the edge of two tall pilsner glasses, and then dip into the salt. Fill the glasses with crushed ice, and reserve the remaining lime wedges for garnish.

Mix the Rose's Lime Juice, beer, and hot sauce together in a pitcher. Pour into the ice-filled glasses, garnish with lime wedges, and serve.

Homemade BBQ Potato Chips

PAT In our house there's always some barbecue going on (even if we're not grilling, we're adding the spice). These chips are dusted with paprika, garlic, sugar, and salt, and once they're out of the fryer, they quickly disappear (so make two batches!).

SERVES 4

Peanut oil, for frying

2 tablespoons paprika

1 tablespoon garlic powder

1 teaspoon sugar

1 teaspoon kosher salt

1 pound russet potatoes (about 2 large), well scrubbed

Preheat the peanut oil in a deep-fryer or Dutch oven to 375 degrees F. (For tips on deep-frying, see page 19.)

Whisk together the paprika, garlic powder, sugar, and salt in a small mixing bowl.

Slice the potatoes into very thin (⅛-inch) slices (you can use a knife, but a mandoline with a straight-blade attachment is helpful).

Fry the potatoes in batches, only a few at a time, for about 3 to 4 minutes. Once they reach a golden-brown color, remove the chips from the fryer and drain on a paper-towel-lined sheet tray. Sprinkle the chips immediately with the barbecue seasoning.

ALTERNATIVE

Baked BBQ Potato Chips

Heat the oven to 400 degrees F.

Toss the potato slices with 3 tablespoons vegetable oil, and season with the barbecue seasoning. Spray two sheet trays with nonstick spray. Arrange the potato slices in a single layer on the prepared sheet trays, leaving some breathing space between them.

Bake for 20 minutes, then start watching the chips closely. After another 5 minutes, they'll start to brown; as soon as you see the browning, take them out of the oven. They turn on a dime from browned to burned!

Frozen Mango Margaritas

PAT At twenty-one, most people want their first cocktail . . . but when our kids are moving a little too fast, we always say, "Slow your roll or pump your brakes, sister!" So Gina came up with this recipe for frozen mango margaritas, which tastes great as written (for us) or with only a splash of the tequila and Cointreau (for Spenser).

MAKES 4 DRINKS

5 lime wedges, and juice of 3 limes

Kosher salt, for rims

One 16-ounce package frozen chunked mango

½ cup good tequila

¼ cup Cointreau

⅓ cup sugar

1½ cups ice cubes

Rub the rim of four glasses with one of the lime wedges. Dip into salt to create a salted rim.

Combine the lime juice, frozen mango, tequila, Cointreau, sugar, and ice cubes in a blender, and purée until smooth. Pour into glasses, and garnish with the remaining four lime wedges. Serve immediately.

February

VALENTINE'S DAY (KEEPING IT SEXY AND LIGHT)

Roasted Tomato and Asparagus Salad

Sexy Seafood Pasta

Chocolate Tartlets

Love Potion #9

WELCOME HOME, BABY! COMING HOME PARTY

Tanya's Spicy Spinach Dip

Smothered Pork Chops

Whipped Garlicky Mashed Potatoes

Green Beans and Bacon (see page 273)

Devil's Food Cake

Valentine's Day (Keeping It Sexy and Light)

A WIFELY PERSPECTIVE: THIS ONE IS SPECIAL

I call it our Lovers' Holiday. Every year I use this day to reflect on our relationship, read old love letters, look at how much we've grown, and ask how we can be and do better.

But here is the key: use the day as a moment to consider and accept that men and women may show their love differently, but the love is there no matter what. Men often express their love by providing, solving our problems, and leading the way. We often express our love through respect, by sharing emotions, and by listening (that's right, without offering advice all the time!). Love is work, no matter what, but the key is to keep working at it with a big dose of compassion.

So, on this night of all nights, cook up some tasty specialties, and your lover will be in seventh heaven. We all know that relationships can be hard, but if you both invest yourselves wholeheartedly, you can usually survive the craziness.

A HUSBAND'S VIEW

Honest to God, I never knew Valentine's Day was so special until Gina and I got together. Growing up in a house with five boys, one girl, and my mother, and coming from humble beginnings, I never really celebrated the day. Sure, my father would get my mother roses or chocolates, but otherwise we just went on our merry way. I remember saving a few quarters and buying a box of heart candies for my (blushing) seventh-grade crush. . . . Today Shelbi buys seven or nine gift boxes for her friends at school—they're even given between girlfriends! I figure this has something to do with the intimacy women share. It didn't take me long to realize how important it was to get myself to the jeweler, and soon it became a mini-Christmas for the girls as well. But, bottom line, it's not what you buy, it's how you seize the day to express your love.

Whether you're dating or have been married one or fifty-one years, you have to keep the romance strong, and in this, even the simple things can be extra special. Celebrate the women in your life—it's their day! After all, you don't see a lot of women ordering flowers at the florist, but there must be forty men in there!

If it were for me, the Valentine's Day menu would be grilled, but this is my

sweetie's day, so a sexy seafood pasta is just the kind of dish she'll love. It's light (if it were heavy, you'd risk putting her to sleep!), a little spicy, and quick and easy. It'll leave you plenty of time to turn on that soft music and reflect, cuddle, and have a romantic evening.

SHELBI'S DIRTY FLOWERS

PAT Gina and I are not big on going out to dinner, because it's too public, so we like to celebrate by doing something quiet at home. However, Gina is such a romantic, she loves to celebrate in style.

I remember a Valentine's Day years ago, in the days when I'd come home late from the restaurant after pulling together barbecue packs for people to take home, and serving couples dining in-house all evening. Shelbi was still small, so Gina had gotten home early. After doing something special for the girls and getting them settled with a video, Gina ran a bath with rose petals for me. Spenser did what her mother said and kept watching the movie, but Shelbi wanted to see what was going on. She came into the bathroom and asked, "Mama, why do you have all those flowers in that bathtub? Are they dirty?" Gina said, "No, they're not dirty. . . . Now, go back upstairs—Daddy's coming home!"

Roasted Tomato and Asparagus Salad

This is what we mean about keeping it light and sexy: we all know asparagus is good for us, but it's also known to be an aphrodisiac. So we're not only enjoying our holiday but we're also paving the road to romance. The smokiness of the roasted tomatoes, the tender crispness of the asparagus, and the bitter and sweet flavors of arugula—all of that says L-O-V-E to us. **SERVES 4**

4 plum tomatoes, halved lengthwise, seeded

½ cup olive oil, divided

½ teaspoon sugar

Kosher salt and freshly ground black pepper to taste

1 small bunch asparagus (about 1 pound), ends trimmed

5 ounces baby arugula

Juice of 1 lemon

3 ounces Parmesan cheese, thinly shaved with a vegetable peeler

Preheat the oven to 425 degrees F. Arrange the racks in the middle of the oven.

Lay the tomatoes out in a single layer in a shallow 2-quart casserole dish. Toss the tomatoes with half of the olive oil, the sugar, salt, and pepper, and then rearrange the tomatoes to make sure they are cut side up. Roast in the oven for 15 minutes.

Remove tomatoes from the oven and arrange the asparagus in a single layer over the tomatoes. Drizzle with the remaining olive oil, and season with salt and pepper. Return the casserole to the oven, and roast for 10 to 12 minutes, until the asparagus is crisp and tender.

Remove the asparagus and tomatoes from the oven, and gently toss (while they are still warm) with the arugula and lemon juice in a large bowl. Season with salt and pepper to taste. Plate each serving, and top with shaved Parmesan. Serve immediately.

NOTE The cooking time for the asparagus will vary depending on their thickness, so keep an eye on them. You don't need to add any more oil to the salad, since the tomatoes are soft and juicy and the vegetables were roasted in oil, which will coat everything just right.

Sexy Seafood Pasta

GINA When we think of romance, we think of something tantalizing and with a little kick. So we created this spicy pasta with just that in mind. Spark up your taste buds with crushed red pepper and roasted tomatoes, and feast your eyes on the jewel-like pink shrimp and shiny black mussel shells nestled in that silky bed of linguine and ribbons of basil leaves. (Ladies, all of this careful planning helps us please our men!) The look of the final dish is just as beautiful at home as it is at a fancy restaurant. Now, what can beat that? **SERVES 4**

Kosher salt

1 pound linguine

2 tablespoons olive oil

2 cloves garlic, minced

1/2 teaspoon crushed red-pepper flakes

1/4 cup dry white wine

One 28-ounce can fire-roasted crushed tomatoes

1/2 pound large shrimp, peeled and deveined

1/2 pound black mussels, scrubbed and cleaned

1/4 cup fresh basil leaves, sliced into ribbons

Bring a large pot of salted water to a boil. Slip the pasta into the boiling water. Cook until al dente.

Pour the oil into a large skillet over medium heat. Once it's hot, toss in the garlic and red-pepper flakes, and cook, stirring, until the garlic is golden and fragrant, just about 1 minute. Pour in the wine and the tomatoes; bring the liquid to a simmer, and allow the sauce to cook for 10 minutes, stirring on occasion.

Stir the shrimp and mussels into the simmering sauce, cover, and cook for 3 minutes, or until the mussels open and the shrimp turns bright pink. (Remove any mussels that have not fully opened.) Give the sauce another stir, and then add the linguine and basil directly to the pan. Toss all together, and serve hot!

Chocolate Tartlets

We're huge fans of these tartlets; while everyone else is sharing a box of chocolates (nice, but dull), we're putting ours in a box you can eat! These tartlets are delicious and beautiful, with a pleasant hint of nuttiness when you add hazelnut liqueur. Topped with chocolate shavings and a dollop of whipped cream, they make a perfect Valentine confection. (We like to make a couple of extra tartlets for the girls—plus, they make great midnight snacks!) **MAKES 5 TARTLETS**

One 18-ounce package refrigerated sugar-cookie dough (recommended: Nestlé Toll House)

5 ounces semisweet chocolate, chopped

¾ cup heavy cream

1 tablespoon hazelnut liqueur

1 tablespoon light corn syrup

1 tablespoon sugar

⅛ teaspoon table salt

1 large egg, at room temperature, beaten

Whipped cream and chocolate shavings, for garnish

Preheat the oven to 350 degrees F.

Coat five 4½-inch tartlet pans with removable bottoms with nonstick spray.

Divide the cookie dough into 5 equal-sized balls. Press each ball into a tartlet pan, making sure they evenly cover the sides and bottoms. Put the pans on a cookie sheet in the oven, and bake for about 15 to 20 minutes, or until the crusts are golden brown. Remove the pans from the oven, and let cool completely.

Turn the oven down to 325 degrees F.

Put the chopped chocolate in a medium heat-proof bowl. Heat the heavy cream and hazelnut liqueur in a small saucepan over low heat, and bring up to a light simmer. Pour the hot cream over the chocolate, and whisk until melted and smooth. Add the corn syrup, sugar, and salt, and whisk in the beaten egg until all the ingredients are combined. Ladle the filling into the cooled tart shells, and bake until the filling is set and the surface is glossy, about 15 to 18 minutes. Remove the tartlets from the oven, and let cool.

Once they're cooled, remove the tartlets from pans and garnish with whipped cream and chocolate shavings.

Welcome Home, Baby! Coming Home Party

WITH LOVE, TANYA

TANYA Gina is my little sister and always will be—even though she thinks that she is grown up because she's married with kids. Pat was always my favorite for her: I have fond memories of when we all would hang out in the "dollhouse," what we'd call Gina's little house in Mississippi, while she and Pat were courting. Gina, Pat, and I would all take turns cooking, and we enjoyed the same kinds of foods. But I think the real reason I love them together is that Pat and I were born on the same day of the year and we really "get" each other—we even like the same movies. I couldn't ask for any more in a brother-in-law. I would do anything for them. When they first got the Food Network show, I didn't hesitate when Gina asked me to pick up and move from Nashville where I'd been catering manager for the Nashville Neely's Barbecue. Moving back to Memphis may not have been my first choice, but I was single with a grown son, and expanding my job to be catering manager for all Neely's Barbecue (taking over what Gina had been doing) meant that I could continue to work in Memphis without skipping a beat. I was in a unique position in the family to help Gina live her dream through *Down Home with the Neelys,* and I've gotten to live the dream with her. I know how hard they work, and I try to help any way I can . . . plus, in true little-sister form, Gina is a "spoiled brat," and I don't mind spoiling her a little more!

GINA Baby, I am not one to travel all the time if I can help it. I guess I'm too much of a homebody, and I like my own things . . . and it's always hard when we hit the road.

Luckily, we got our own Tanya. Everybody needs their "own" somebody, who can make everything all right. Tanya works with us and always has a place at our table. And when we travel—whether it's for a book tour, a festival, or an appearance—Tanya has cooked up all our favorites when we get home. What a nice thing to come home to . . . and what a great excuse for a holiday. Forget those mints and little chocolates; when you look at this menu, you'll see why we're always running back to our house, never wanting to leave again.

Tanya's Spicy Spinach Dip

If you're a Ro*tel lover, then this is your dish. (In case you aren't familiar, it's a blend of diced tomatoes with green chiles, often used to make a mean *chili con queso.*) We love how Tanya adds spinach to her version of this popular Southern dip, so it makes us feel healthy and good even though it's still a "comfort" food. We're typically starving upon arrival, and a great spicy spinach dip with a bowl of tortilla chips is a good way to take the edge off. Throw your luggage down and dig in!

SERVES 4 TO 6

2 tablespoons butter

1 small onion, chopped

2 cloves garlic, chopped

2 tablespoons all-purpose flour

1 cup heavy cream

Two 10-ounce boxes frozen chopped spinach, thawed and drained

One 10-ounce can diced tomatoes with green chilies, preferably Ro*tel

1 cup shredded Monterey Jack cheese

Kosher salt

Melt the butter in a medium saucepan set over medium heat. Once it foams, toss in the onion and garlic, and sauté until softened, about 3 minutes. Sprinkle in the flour, and cook, stirring, until it becomes a light-blond color. Slowly stir in the heavy cream, and bring the sauce to a simmer; cook until it starts to thicken, about 5 minutes. Stir in the spinach, Ro*tel, and cheese, and cook until the cheese is melted. Season to taste with salt.

Pour the dip into a serving bowl and serve warm with tortilla chips.

Whipped Garlicky Mashed Potatoes

GINA Who doesn't like a good potato? I know I married a meat-and-potatoes man, and so does Tanya. She always finds a way to make great potatoes, and these are some of her very best. Buttery and garlicky—yum.

PAT Baby, you can't do pork chops without mashed potatoes. There's something about taking your fork and getting a bite of pork chop and garlic mashed potatoes at the same time. You just take both of those jokers and let 'em hit the palate!

SERVES 4

2 pounds Yukon Gold potatoes, peeled and cubed

Kosher salt

3 tablespoons butter

3/4 cup heavy cream

6 cloves garlic, minced

Freshly ground black pepper

Plop the potatoes into a large pot of cold water. Add a generous pinch of salt, bring it to a boil, then reduce the pot to a simmer, and cook until fork-tender, about 20 minutes. Drain the pot, and reserve the potatoes.

Combine the butter, cream, and garlic in the empty pot, and stir over medium heat, until the butter melts and the garlic is slightly cooked, 2 or 3 minutes. Put the potatoes back into the pot, and remove from heat. Use an electric hand mixer on medium speed to mash and whip the potatoes together until smooth. Add salt and pepper to taste, and whip again to combine. Serve immediately.

Devil's Food Cake

GINA This is my absolute favorite cake. Tanya has been baking it for me since I was a little girl—which I was yesterday. . . . I can remember when my sister Kim made it for her boyfriend, Tony, who is now her husband. I watched her in that kitchen, baking with such love and care. I begged for a small piece and she said, "No, it's Tony's birthday." So I sat on that stool and swung my feet and waited and waited.

It got pretty dark, and Kim was no longer smiling—she'd gotten that evil look on her face that we all have had at one time or another. The wait went on, and then . . . ding-dong. He'd finally arrived, and Kim was all fired up to give him a piece of her mind for being so late. After some loud, angry whispering between Kim and Tony at the front door, Kim took my beautiful, coveted cake, went straight out the door, and threw it into the garbage can outside! I screamed and stood by that can in shock, but Tanya made me come in, and baked me another one just to shut me up. (Hence, you can see where my "spoiledness" comes from, and the reason Tanya knows it's my favorite.)

Now we all love this cake. I am a true chocolate lover, and adding more chocolate on top—really, what more can you say? But you know Pat—he likes to reach into the freezer and throw a big scoop of vanilla on top of his slice. **SERVES 10**

CAKE

3 large eggs, at room temperature

3/4 cup (1 1/2 sticks) unsalted butter, melted

1 1/2 cups warm water

1 cup Dutch-process cocoa powder

2 cups all-purpose flour, sifted

1 3/4 cups granulated sugar

1 1/2 teaspoons baking powder

1/2 teaspoon baking soda

1/2 teaspoon table salt

FROSTING

1/2 cup unsalted butter

3 ounces semisweet chocolate, chopped

Preheat the oven to 350 degrees F.

Spray two 8-inch cake pans with 1 1/2-inch sides lightly with cooking spray. Arrange racks in the middle of the oven.

Beat the eggs, butter, water, and cocoa powder together in a large bowl in a standing mixer until smooth. Whisk the flour, sugar, baking powder, baking soda, and salt together in a second bowl. Add the dry mixture to the wet ingredients, and beat until evenly blended and smooth, 2 to 3 minutes, scraping down the sides with a spatula.

Divide the batter between the two greased pans. Bake for 30 to 35 minutes, or until a toothpick inserted into the center of the cake comes out clean.

Cool in pans for 5 minutes before turning out onto wire cooling rack. Cool completely before frosting.

For the frosting: Heat the butter and chocolate in a heavy-bottomed saucepan over moderate heat. Stir constantly with a rubber spatula

¼ cup Dutch-process cocoa powder

1½ teaspoons pure vanilla extract

2 cups confectioners' sugar, whisked or sifted

⅔ cup sour cream

until the mixture is smooth and melted. Remove the saucepan from the heat, and whisk in the cocoa powder and vanilla until the mixture is smooth and the cocoa is dissolved. Beat in confectioners' sugar and sour cream with a hand mixer, beating until smooth and creamy.

To assemble the cake: Place one layer, top side down, on a cake stand. Spread on it a thick layer of frosting with a spatula. Place the next layer of cake right side up on top of the frosting. Frost the top and sides of the cake by working from the center of the cake toward the edge, making sure to coat evenly.

March

MARCH MADNESS

Fresh Mango Salsa and Homemade Tortilla Chips

Southern-Style Fish Tacos with Crunchy Slaw and Chipotle Mayo

Blackberry Mojitos

MOVIE NIGHT

Memphis-Style Popcorn

Gina's Favorite Chicken and Spinach Pizza

Ice Cream Sundaes with Homemade Bourbon-Caramel-Pecan Sauce

HAPPY HOUR

Crab-Stuffed Mushroom Caps

Drunken Goat Cheese and Tomato Mini-Sandwiches

Devils on Horseback

Gina's Gin Cooler

March Madness

GINA HAS A BALL

GINA Now, I have already told you guys that I am not into sports, but to illustrate this point, let me tell you a story.

Me being me, I never realized that there was such a thing as "basketball etiquette." So picture Pat and me sitting courtside at a Memphis Grizzlies game. The game has started, and I'm just running my mouth (as usual), when the ball rolls toward my feet. Jason Kidd of the Dallas Mavericks was on the court, so I looked way up and asked him if I could shoot the ball. Jason was like, "Yeah, shoot it." Then the crowd started yelling, "Shoot it! Shoot it!" So I stood up, took my crazy self out there in my heels, and dribbled that ball and aimed toward the goal—I mean basket. . . . Of course it didn't go in, but the whole crowd was yelling.

Now Pat looks at me and says, "Are you crazy? You aren't supposed to go out there; you can get ejected from the game!" And I said, "By who?," and he pointed out the referee, "the man in the striped shirt." *Oh* . . . you should have seen how that man was looking back at me. I said, "Aw, okay. I didn't know people got so testy about it." So I turned to Jason and said, "You got me in trouble. I should beat you up!" and he is just laughing hysterically. Then guess what? The ball comes my way again, and I pick it up. Everybody is yelling again, "Shoot it, shoot it!" I look over at the referee this time, and he is looking at me with an air of defeat, as if to say, "Shoot it if you want to." But instead, I carried the ball over to him, personally.

PAT Fellas, this one is for you, or better yet, it's for us. There's nothing that I look forward to more than NCAA basketball. Any time you have great ball games, with all the excitement and something great to munch on, you're pretty much into my version of full-blown March Madness. It's rare that I get to call the shots in household entertainment. But during March Madness, no one argues with me—the whole month is mine.

In Memphis, the temperature in March is already into the high seventies and eighties, so Gina's idea is to keep the menu on the light, seasonal side. And remember: there's four quarters in a game, and sometimes doubleheaders, so you might be sipping and munching all day. The finger-type food fits the mood—especially when the Neely boys get together, 'cause "there's a lotta ruckus in the roomas," as my mother would say.

GINA How I feel about sports doesn't get in the way of wanting my sweetie and his friends to have a good time with a great menu. And this is a great menu. Initially those big, burly men thought fish tacos were too healthy an alternative, because they were so stuck on their nachos and wings. But one bite was all the convincing they needed for this "outside the box" game-day menu.

Fresh Mango Salsa and Homemade Tortilla Chips

GINA My attraction to mangoes was confirmed on a trip Pat and I took to Mexico. The velvety fruit tastes like an exotic mix of pineapples and peaches, and the flavor just explodes in your mouth. In creating this salsa, I stuck with Mexican tradition and added fresh cilantro, which you can chop or tear apart. Cilantro also offers a health benefit by soothing the digestive system. So, little do the guys know, I'm taking care of their stomachs as well as their appetite! (Ladies, y'all can thank me later.)

Mind you, I was a little skeptical about whether they'd go for it, so I deep-fried the tortilla chips, so they'd have something familiar to dip. **SERVES 4 TO 6**

2 mangoes, peeled, chopped into ½-inch chunks

2 plum tomatoes, seeded, diced

1 small red onion, diced

¼ cup chopped fresh cilantro

1 jalapeño, ribs and seeds removed, minced

2 cloves garlic, minced

Juice of 2 limes

Kosher salt

Combine the mangoes, tomatoes, red onion, cilantro, jalapeño, garlic, and lime juice in a bowl. Season with salt, and toss. Let stand for 15 minutes before serving, so the flavors can marry.

TORTILLA CHIPS

SERVES 4 TO 6

Peanut oil, for frying

10 corn tortillas

Kosher salt

Heat the peanut oil in a large Dutch oven or deep-fryer to 350 degrees F. (For tips on deep-frying, see page 19.)

Arrange the corn tortillas in a stack, and cut into six equal wedges. Drop the tortillas into the oil, in batches, and fry until crisp and golden, about 1½ to 2 minutes.

Remove the chips from the fryer and place on a paper-towel-lined sheet tray. Sprinkle the chips immediately with the salt, and serve warm with the salsa.

ALTERNATIVE

Baked Tortilla Chips

Heat the oven to 350 degrees F.

Lightly brush both sides of the tortillas with a few tablespoons of vegetable oil. Stack a few corn tortillas at a time, and cut through the stack to make each tortilla into six equal wedges. Spread the wedges out in a single layer on two baking sheets, season with salt, and bake for 15 minutes, or until crisp and golden.

Southern-Style Fish Tacos with Crunchy Slaw and Chipotle Mayo

GINA Fish tacos—you gotta love them. But of course seafood has always been my thing.

The key to this dish lies in the freshness of your coleslaw. You can always use store-bought, but our recipe is so quick, and making it fresh adds a crispness that I'm not too sure store-bought can provide. Also, the jalapeño pepper in the slaw, combined with the chipotle mayo, makes our slaw smoky and spicy!

I think catfish works better than other fish, because it has a good way of standing up to the heat of the frying pan . . . plus, I just love the flavor. This may be because our family had a tradition of eating catfish every Friday night for dinner. (We were probably making fish tacos before they got a fancy reputation.) And I have this thing about wraps—because you can pile everything into them and then just munch it down. **MAKES 8 TACOS**

CRUNCHY SLAW

2 tablespoons freshly squeezed lime juice

1 tablespoon canola oil

1 tablespoon honey

Kosher salt

1 cup finely shredded green cabbage

1 cup finely shredded red cabbage

½ small red onion, minced

1 small jalapeño, seeds and veins removed, minced

2 tablespoons finely chopped fresh cilantro

CHIPOTLE MAYO

1 cup mayonnaise

1 chipotle pepper packed in adobo sauce

2 teaspoons adobo sauce

2 teaspoons honey

(continued)

For the slaw: Whisk the lime juice, oil, honey, and salt together in a bowl. Add the green and red cabbage, red onion, jalapeño, and cilantro, and toss to combine. Cover with plastic wrap, and let the bowl chill in the fridge for 1 hour, so the flavors can develop.

For the chipotle mayo: Blend the mayonnaise, chipotle pepper, adobo sauce, and honey in a food processor until smooth. Remove from processor, and set aside until ready to serve.

For the catfish: Heat 2 inches of oil in a Dutch oven to 375 degrees F. (For tips on deep-frying, see page 19.)

Slice the catfish into 1-inch-thick fingers on a diagonal, and season with salt and pepper. Whisk together the buttermilk, egg, and hot sauce on a rimmed plate. Stir together the cornmeal, flour, garlic powder, and cayenne pepper on another rimmed plate, and season with salt and pepper. Working in batches, dip the catfish into the buttermilk batter, then dredge it through the cornmeal mixture, shaking off the excess.

When the oil is hot, gently drop the catfish into the Dutch oven and fry until golden brown, working in batches, about 2 to 3 minutes per batch. Remove to a paper-towel-lined sheet tray when done, and immediately season with salt and pepper.

CATFISH

Peanut oil, for frying

Two 6-ounce catfish fillets

Kosher salt and freshly ground
    black pepper

1 cup buttermilk

1 egg, beaten

2 tablespoons hot sauce, preferably
    Tabasco

$\frac{1}{2}$ cup yellow cornmeal

$\frac{1}{2}$ cup all-purpose flour

1 teaspoon garlic powder

$\frac{1}{2}$ teaspoon cayenne pepper

8 corn tortillas

Lime wedges, for garnish

Fresh cilantro sprigs, for garnish

Place the tortillas on a plate, and wrap the plate with damp paper towels. Microwave on high for 45 seconds. (Alternatively, if you have a gas stove, turn the heat to medium and place a corn tortilla directly over the flame, to toast for about 15 seconds on each side. This will soften the tortilla and give it a delicious smoky flavor.)

To assemble the tacos, place a generous portion of fried catfish onto the center of a warmed tortilla. Top with the crunchy slaw, and top with chipotle mayonnaise. Garnish with lime wedges and cilantro.

ALTERNATIVE

GRILLED CATFISH

Preheat a grill or grill pan to medium-high heat.

Slice the catfish into 1-inch-thick fingers on the diagonal. Brush with a few tablespoons olive oil on each side, and season with salt and pepper.

Grill the catfish 2 to 3 minutes per side. Assemble the tacos as directed.

Blackberry Mojitos

GINA The Cubans had the right idea when they invented the classic mojito: it really is a perfect cocktail (not too sweet, not too sour).

Another great thing about mojitos is that you can add almost any flavor to them and they taste amazing. I was experimenting with mojitos, creating a brown-sugar one, and I thought, why not blackberries? I've always been a fan of blackberries: I even like to eat them frozen right out of the freezer. (I do the same thing with grapes.) The infusion of mint and basil gives this version an herbal freshness, and the agave nectar is a gentle, natural sweetener that dissolves quickly. Of course, you can leave out the rum and just pour some soda water on top of the berries, but why would you? Either way, the drink is a beautiful spring color, and spring is my favorite season, when everything is blooming, and life's possibilities seem endless.

MAKES 4 DRINKS

One 5-ounce container blackberries

1 medium lime, cut into wedges

10 fresh mint leaves, torn

6 fresh basil leaves, torn

¼ cup agave nectar

6 ounces light rum

Soda water, chilled

Muddle the blackberries, lime, mint, and basil with a wooden spoon in the bottom of a small glass pitcher. Stir in the agave nectar and rum.

Divide the mixture between four ice-filled glasses, and top with soda water. Stir with a cocktail spoon and enjoy.

Movie Night

GINA Full disclosure: I am an undercover couch potato. My secret vice: Movie Night. I'd go to the theater more, but my schedule is so crazy that I usually end up waiting for movies to come out on DVD. But then I get my barbecue popcorn, and a glass of champagne, and nobody better talk to me, not even Pat. I love movies so much that I often find myself quoting movie lines. Ask any of my family or friends—you can even ask Whoopi on *The View,* because I was quoting *The Color Purple* to her, and she called me "special"! I laugh about that to this day, because I couldn't help being myself; once I got talking about that movie, I couldn't stop!

Give me *Lady Day, What Ever Happened to Baby Jane?, Mommie Dearest,* and mix it up with a little *Love Jones, The Best Man, A Soldier's Story* . . . Oh, honey, this list can get way too long. But watching movies is my favorite way to relax and truly remove myself from the craziness of everyday life. Often I see myself in so many of the characters I enjoy watching. If you're a fan of old movies, check out Bette Davis in *All About Eve:* "Fasten your seatbelts, it's going to be a bumpy night!" (I can relate to her ability to predict when trouble's a-brewin'!)

Have I convinced all of you to try this out? Well, Pat has some advice he'd like to share for any male Movie Night skeptics out there. . . .

PAT You can get to a very contented place watching movies with your family, and the beauty of it all is that you never have to leave home. I've become something of a pro, having watched *Steel Magnolias* more times than I care to remember, because that's the movie my wife and daughters wanted to see. I know what you're thinking: big guy like me watching chick flicks? All I can say is, don't be afraid to give it a go—you might learn a few things.

To make the most of Movie Night, you've got to have some munchies. And I don't care how great the movie is, it's just not the same without popcorn. In our house, we fire up Memphis-style popcorn (simply can't beat it). And then Mama's gotta have her favorite pizza—Gina's includes chunks of grilled chicken and fresh spinach. To keep that Movie Night train a-movin', we finish the evening with ice cream topped with a little caramel-pecan sauce. It's a dessert that will make you kick your shoes off and rub your feet together.

Ice Cream Sundaes with Homemade Bourbon-Caramel-Pecan Sauce

Is there really anything else to say? The keywords are "bourbon," "caramel," "pecan"! Oh, and "ice cream sundae"! Done. **MAKES 2 CUPS OF SAUCE, 6 TO 8 SUNDAES**

½ cup water

1 cup sugar

1 cup heavy cream

3 tablespoons butter

2 tablespoons bourbon

¼ cup coarsely chopped pecans

Pinch of kosher salt

1 quart vanilla ice cream

Pour the water into a large saucepan. Whisk in the sugar, and bring to a boil. Boil until it becomes a deep-golden-brown color, about 8 minutes. Remove it from the heat as soon as it's reached this color, or it will burn.

Heat the heavy cream in another saucepan until warm. Then carefully whisk the cream into the caramel mixture until smooth (the mixture will bubble vigorously!). When the bubbling subsides, stir in the butter, bourbon, pecans, and a pinch of salt. Let the mixture cool slightly.

Scoop the ice cream into serving dishes, and top with the warm caramel sauce. Enjoy immediately.

Happy Hour

GINA I often wonder—where do you think Happy Hour originated? It's almost as good as Ladies' Day/Night Out. So I bet it was invented by a hardworking woman looking for a pleasurable hour to escape and relax each day.

We've always loved Happy Hour, because it gives us time to catch up with each other and catch our breath after a workday. When Pat was at the restaurant and I was at the bank, I couldn't wait to get out of there by the end of the day. It was a running joke at work: I'd say, "If you guys make me late meeting my husband, you're going on my bad list." So, once everything was wrapped, and the vault closed, I'd race to meet Pat. He would always have my drink ready. (That was the rule—whoever got there first ordered.) No matter what had happened that day, the company of my husband coupled with the first sip of that cocktail washed it away. Then we would talk about our day, and get a laugh out of the funny parts.

But since our TV show launched, all that has changed. Now when we go out, people want to strike up a conversation and ask us questions. And as much as we love our fans, it's not quite the same as it was when it was just the two of us. If I beat Pat to the bar, I'll tell whoever comes up to chat, "That info is gonna cost you a cocktail!" And that used to discourage people, but they usually don't mind picking up the tab anymore. So we had to bring the Happy Hour to a local place where no one can find us: H-O-M-E.

And guess what? We love it even better now. No interruptions, no shoptalk (most of the time): just the quiet of our home and the lush greenness of the back-yard. People ask us all the time, "Why do you guys stay home so much?" I always say, "Even though it's a blessing, try stepping in these pumps!" There's only so long I can be out with my stilettos and my business face on. Compared with that, Happy Hour at home sweet home is fuzzy piggie slippers.

Crab-Stuffed Mushroom Caps

PAT This being Happy Hour, we've gotta have crab-stuffed mushrooms. And any time I can get Gina to eat mushrooms with me, I do! (Guys, let me tell you, I've been told mushrooms are an aphrodisiac, so when the guests leave it might be time for *your* Happy Hour!) **SERVES 6**

24 large (about 2-inch-diameter) mushrooms

2 tablespoons butter, plus 2 tablespoons melted butter

1 shallot, finely diced

2 cloves garlic, minced

Pinch of crushed red-pepper flakes

½ cup panko bread crumbs

2 tablespoons finely chopped fresh parsley

Kosher salt and freshly ground black pepper to taste

½ cup mayonnaise

1 tablespoon Dijon mustard

2 tablespoons finely grated Parmesan cheese

1 egg, lightly beaten

Juice of ½ lemon

Dash of hot sauce, preferably Tabasco

8 ounces lump crabmeat

Heat your oven to 350 degrees F.

Remove the mushroom stems, and coarsely chop them.

Melt 2 tablespoons butter in a medium sauté pan set over medium heat. Once the butter foams, add the chopped mushroom stems, shallot, garlic, and red-pepper flakes, and sauté until tender, about 4 minutes. Pour the panko and parsley into the pan, and season with salt and pepper. Stir to coat with the butter. Remove from heat, and let cool slightly.

Combine the mayonnaise, Dijon mustard, cheese, egg, lemon juice, hot sauce, salt, and pepper in a medium bowl. Stir in the mushroom mixture, then gently fold in the crabmeat, being careful not to break up lumps of crabmeat (they taste good!).

Spread the mushroom caps on a sheet pan lined with aluminum foil. Brush both sides of the mushroom caps with the melted butter, and season with salt and pepper. Fill each cap with a generous spoonful of the crab mixture. Bake for 20 minutes, until the mushrooms are hot and tender.

NOTE If you have some leftover filling, you can fill a small ramekin and top with Parmesan cheese for an easy gratin dip.

Drunken Goat Cheese and Tomato Mini-Sandwiches

PAT Gina introduced me to drunken goat cheese, and if you haven't had it, you haven't had cheese. (You can find it at Whole Foods and other fine food stores.) Drunken goat is semifirm and cured in red wine, so it has a maroon-colored skin. Flavorful and smooth, it goes great on a ripe-tomato sandwich. If you don't have softened butter at the ready, a good shortcut is to spread plain mayonnaise on the outsides of the sandwiches instead. They'll fry up just as crisp and golden as they will with butter. **SERVES 6 TO 8**

Sixteen 1/2-inch-thick slices Pullman-style white bread, crusts removed

6 tablespoons butter, softened

8 ounces drunken goat cheese or other aged cheese, grated

Sun-dried-tomato mayonnaise (recipe follows)

Heat a large skillet or a griddle over medium-low heat.

Place eight slices of bread on your work surface. Spread butter on one side of each slice of bread. Divide the cheese between the eight slices of bread. Spread the sun-dried mayo on the remaining eight slices of bread, and place on top of cheese slices, mayonnaise side down. Butter the top side of each sandwich. Cook the sandwiches, in batches, until the bread begins to turn golden brown and the cheese is starting to melt, about 5 minutes. Turn the sandwiches over with a spatula, and cook the other side, another 3 or 4 minutes more.

Remove the sandwiches from the pan, slice each into four triangles, and serve.

SUN-DRIED-TOMATO MAYO

MAKES ABOUT 1 1/4 CUPS

1 cup mayonnaise

1/4 cup sun-dried tomatoes packed in oil, drained

1 clove garlic, smashed and peeled

2 tablespoons freshly squeezed lemon juice

Kosher salt and freshly ground black pepper

Dash of hot sauce, preferably Tabasco

Process the mayonnaise, sun-dried tomatoes, garlic, lemon juice, salt, pepper, and hot sauce in a food processor until smooth.

Devils on Horseback

"Devils on Horseback" are an old Southern favorite, and it's hard to believe how so much flavor can be packed into one little bite. We like to make a double batch whenever we're having a family party; they fly off the plate so fast we can barely keep up! Luckily, they're just as easy to make as they are to eat. There are several variations that are fun to try: for example, try substituting Parmesan for the blue cheese, or dates for the prunes. **SERVES 6**

24 large pitted prunes

½-pound block Danish blue cheese, cut into bite-sized cubes

9 slices bacon, cut crosswise into thirds

Toothpicks, soaked in water for 10 minutes

2 teaspoons smoked paprika

Place the oven rack in the middle of the oven, and preheat to 450 degrees F.

Stuff each prune with a cube of blue cheese. Wrap a piece of bacon around each prune, covering the cheese so it can't escape once baked. Use the toothpick to secure the bacon.

Place the bacon-wrapped prunes on a sheet tray lined with a wire rack, and sprinkle with the smoked paprika.

Bake for 15 to 20 minutes, or until the bacon is crisp. Let cool a few minutes before serving.

Gina's Gin Cooler

PAT Gina will mix up a batch of this for me to serve our guests, and if I'm lucky she'll make enough for me, too. It's *good.* **MAKES 1 COCKTAIL**

Five ⅛-inch-thick slices peeled cucumber, plus one ¼-inch-thick slice for garnish

8 torn mint leaves, plus 1 mint sprig for garnish

Juice of 1 lime

1 tablespoon light-brown sugar

2 ounces gin

½ cup club soda, chilled

Muddle together the five cucumber slices, the torn mint, the lime juice, and brown sugar in a cocktail shaker. Add the gin, and fill with ice. Shake vigorously, and strain into an ice-filled highball glass. Top with club soda. Garnish with a cucumber wheel and a sprig of mint.

April

EASTER SUNDAY

Simple Deviled Eggs

Pat's Grilled Leg of Lamb with Mint Vinaigrette

Buttered and Spiced Spring Peas

Roasted Red Potatoes

Angel Biscuits

Banana Cake with Coconut Frosting

SPRING CLEANING PARTY

One-Handed Turkey Burgers

Grilled Potato Wedges

Chewy Pecan Bars

Minted Iced Tea

REHEARSAL DINNER

Fried Catfish

Hush Puppies

Mustard Slaw

Peach Spritzer

Shot of Love

Easter Sunday

GINA Our Easter Sunday tradition started with my great-great-grandmother. In her world, you didn't miss church ever (unless you were on your deathbed). There was regular service, then afternoon and evening Bible study, and *vacation* Bible school. Our church had an elaborate pageant every Easter; our whole family would be sitting in the front row in our Sunday finest, watching the whole thing. It was one of those instances where you better not fudge a line, or else the family would tease you about it forever. There'd be rehearsals upon rehearsals, but, no matter what, I'd always forget a line.

I continued the tradition with my girls. It was a big deal to go and purchase an Easter dress, shoes, purses, and special bows or bonnets. And wouldn't you know it, Spenser would always forget a line in the program, too, so I'd be front and center mouthing it to her—didn't matter; she was getting teased. After church, we had the big Easter-egg hunt before the family dinner. The goal was to find the "golden egg" with money in it, and I'd always try to sneak my girls in that direction, just as my sisters did with me!

PAT My brothers and I couldn't wait for those long Easter services to end. (We called it "All Day Church.") We would worship in our new Easter outfits, then rush home, change clothes, and head to Mama Daisy's house for an egg hunt and a fantastic meal. Our grandfather, Daddy Milton, would also go home and change—but then he'd run out to the front porch and light up a big cigar!

Fast-forward two generations, and our mothers and siblings usually end up at our house. After church, and after dinner has been prepared, I keep Daddy Milton's tradition alive by going out into the backyard, firing up a big cigar, and settling down to reflect. Daddy Milton knew how to celebrate Easter Sunday.

Simple Deviled Eggs

GINA If you are having an Easter-egg hunt, you might as well have deviled eggs. I remember asking my great-great-grandmother, "Why do they call them devil eggs?" And she replied, "Because if you eat too many, the devil will show up!" To this day, I have never understood that saying, but I miss all those little pearls of wisdom that my mom and grandmother used to share. The two of them were magic together, and they always kept us guessing. Pat had a similar experience: as a child, he always wondered how his mother got the insides of the hard-boiled egg out, made a delicious egg mixture, then put it back in!

Deviled eggs are easy and even fun to make with the kids. Here, once again, I do my thing as the "Spice Fairy" with a magic sprinkling of black and red pepper, which gives this dish just the right amount of *kick*. **MAKES 24 DEVILED EGGS**

12 large eggs, hard-boiled

⅓ cup mayonnaise

1 tablespoon Dijon mustard

1 tablespoon dill-pickle relish

1 tablespoon freshly squeezed lemon juice

¼ teaspoon cayenne pepper

Kosher salt and freshly ground black pepper

Fresh chives, finely sliced, for garnish

Peel and halve the hard-boiled eggs, and remove the yolks to a small bowl. Add the mayonnaise, Dijon mustard, relish, lemon juice, cayenne, salt, and pepper to the bowl, and mash everything together with a wooden spoon until smooth. Pipe the filling back into the egg halves with a frosting bag with a large star tip (or spoon it in with a teaspoon). Sprinkle with chives.

NOTE To avoid pockmarked eggs, use older eggs. They are generally easier to peel than fresh, and I hate peeling eggs!

How to Make Perfect Hard-Boiled Eggs

Place the eggs in a large saucepan, and cover with cold water. Once the pot has come to a boil, cover the pot and remove from the heat; let the eggs sit in the water for 14 minutes. Rinse under cold water, then peel.

Pat's Grilled Leg of Lamb with Mint Vinaigrette

GINA Now, you guys know I am married to the "grill master"—and yet we never seem to think of grilling lamb! Adding the mint vinaigrette pulls the whole thing together in the best possible way: the piquant flavor of the vinaigrette contrasts perfectly with the earthy smoked lamb. It's a grilled twist on a classic Easter dish.

PAT Y'all know how I feel about my grill. She loves it when I bring her different types of meats so we can cook them to perfection. Letting these beautiful cuts of lamb soak in the marinade overnight ensures a delicious flavor, and once Gina adds her outstanding mint vinaigrette, there is nothing else for these babies to do but make it to your plate. **SERVES 6 TO 8**

One 7-pound leg of lamb, bone-in, trimmed of excess fat (you can have your butcher do this for you)

½ cup buttermilk

¼ cup Dijon mustard

2 tablespoons olive oil, plus more for the grill

6 cloves garlic, minced

2 tablespoons chopped fresh rosemary leaves

Juice of 1 lemon

1 tablespoon kosher salt

2 teaspoons freshly ground black pepper

1 recipe mint vinaigrette (recipe follows)

Place the lamb in a large ceramic baking dish or roasting pan.

Combine the buttermilk, mustard, olive oil, garlic, rosemary, lemon juice, and salt and pepper in a small bowl. Rub the mixture all over the lamb, cover with plastic wrap, and place in the fridge. Let marinate for 12 hours or overnight.

Remove the lamb from the fridge to allow it to come up to room temperature.

Rub the grill grates with an oil-coated paper towel. Heat your grill to medium-high, using charcoal or gas. Place the lamb on the grill away from the flame (using indirect heat). Grill, covered, turning periodically, for 1 hour 15 minutes, or until a thermometer inserted into the thickest part of the lamb (without touching bone) reads 135 degrees F.

Remove the lamb from the grill, and loosely cover with foil. Allow to rest for 20 minutes before carving. Carve by holding the lamb up vertically by the bone and slicing down, across the grain, into thin slices. Spread slices on a platter, and drizzle with the mint vinaigrette.

MINT VINAIGRETTE

MAKES ABOUT 1¼ CUPS

1 small shallot, minced

⅓ cup finely chopped fresh mint

¼ cup rice-wine vinegar

Juice of 1 lemon

½ cup extra-virgin olive oil

½ teaspoon crushed red-pepper
    flakes

Kosher salt and freshly ground
    black pepper

Whisk together the shallot, mint, vinegar, and lemon juice in a small bowl. Whisk in the olive oil, and season with red-pepper flakes, salt, and pepper.

Buttered and Spiced Spring Peas

It's springtime, y'all! So—sauté these peas in butter with onions, and a hit of red-pepper flakes, and your kitchen will fill with the smells of this wonderful season. It'll put you and your guests in a happy mood and put a spring in everybody's step.

SERVES 6

1 pound fresh shelled peas or frozen peas, thawed

Kosher salt and freshly ground black pepper

2 tablespoons butter

½ small onion, finely chopped

¼ teaspoon crushed red-pepper flakes

If you're using fresh peas, cook them in a pot of boiling salted water for 3 or 4 minutes, until just tender. Drain in a colander. (If using frozen peas, skip this step.)

Melt the butter in a large sauté pan set over medium-high heat. Add the onion and red-pepper flakes, and cook, stirring, until the onion is tender, about 4 minutes. Pour in the cooked or thawed frozen peas, and sauté until heated through, about 3 more minutes. Season with salt and pepper.

Roasted Red Potatoes

PAT Gina loves the daintiness of these "baby reds," and the garlic, rosemary, and olive oil pop on your palate. But Spenser and Shelbi inherited their need for some potatoes with most meals from their daddy. We love us some taters.   **SERVES 6**

3 pounds small red potatoes, well scrubbed

4 large cloves garlic

¼ cup extra-virgin olive oil

3 tablespoons roughly chopped fresh rosemary leaves

Kosher salt and freshly ground black pepper

Preheat the oven to 450 degrees F.

Spread the potatoes on a large rimmed sheet tray, and toss them with the garlic, olive oil, rosemary, salt, and pepper. Roast for 35 minutes, until golden and crisp, shaking the tray a couple of times during the cooking process to turn them over.

Banana Cake with Coconut Frosting

How delicious is a banana cake with coconut frosting? Can you say, "Beat me down, this is so *good*"?

This recipe is all about the bananas, so try and find the very-well-ripened bananas. They are sweeter and softer, and definitely add more banana taste to the cake. Of course, the real star of this cake is the coconut frosting. Once they eat this dessert, your family and guests will have found the golden egg, and you just might get a standing ovation. Happy Easter! **SERVES 12**

2 sticks (1 cup) butter, at room temperature, plus more for pans

2½ cups all-purpose flour, plus more for the pans

1 teaspoon baking powder

½ teaspoon baking soda

1 teaspoon table salt

3 large very ripe bananas

1½ cups sugar

2 large eggs

½ cup sour cream

2 teaspoons pure vanilla extract

¾ cup chopped pecans

2 cups sweetened coconut flakes, for garnish

1 recipe coconut frosting (recipe follows)

Preheat the oven to 350 degrees F, and adjust the rack to the middle shelf. Butter and flour two 9-inch cake pans.

Whisk together the flour, baking powder, baking soda, and salt in a large bowl. Mash the bananas with a wooden spoon in a separate, small bowl, leaving a bit of texture.

Cream the butter and sugar together in the bowl of a standing mixer until light and fluffy. Crack in the eggs, one at a time, mixing in the first completely before adding the second. Stir in the mashed bananas, sour cream, and vanilla, and beat until just combined. Add the dry ingredients, and gently stir in the pecans. Divide the batter between the two pans.

Bake for 25 to 28 minutes, or until a toothpick inserted into the center comes out clean. Let cool for 10 minutes in the pan, then turn out onto a wire rack to cool completely.

While the cakes are cooling, pour coconut flakes evenly onto a baking sheet. Place in the 350-degree oven and toast for 2 to 3 minutes, or until they turn a light-golden-brown color.

To assemble the cakes: Place one layer, top side down, on a cake stand. Spread on a thick layer of frosting with a spatula. Place the other layer of cake on top of the frosting. Frost the top and sides of the cake by working from the center of the cake toward the edge, making sure to coat evenly. Gently press the toasted coconut on the sides of the cake.

NOTE To ripen the bananas quickly, put them in a paper bag and fold the bag closed. The bananas should be ripe and ready for cooking in 2 days.

COCONUT FROSTING

MAKES 7½ CUPS

Two 8-ounce packages cream
cheese, softened

½ cup (1 stick) unsalted butter,
softened

2 teaspoons pure vanilla extract

¾ teaspoon coconut extract

5 cups confectioners' sugar

Beat the cream the cheese and butter together in a standing mixer until light and smooth. Pour in the vanilla and coconut extracts, and slowly add the confectioners' sugar, 1 cup at a time, until thoroughly incorporated, scraping down the sides of the bowl with a spatula as needed. Set aside until ready to frost.

Spring Cleaning Party

PAT Mama Neely was a firm believer in spring cleaning. And, boy oh boy, did I come to dread that day. One spring in particular, she really went crazy. Turning to my brothers and me, she said she wanted us to paint the whole house. I was maybe twelve; Gaelin, the oldest, was probably twenty—with Mark and Tony in between. (Of course, Chris, the baby of the family, got out of most of the work.) It was already pretty damn hot, and I remember looking up at the house and wondering, "How in hell are we going to paint this?" I was young for such an important task, but that wasn't the worst of it. You see, she wanted the house painted hot pink with red trim! She had five boys and she wanted a pink house! Gaelin and Tony had the most experience, so they did the trim work, while Mark and I rolled. I actually found myself enjoying the work, and in about two weeks, we had finished. I still remember how proud we all felt when Mom came out and said, "Great job!" (Man, how times have changed. Spenser and Shelbi would run away before they'd paint a closet!) The paint job may have been a one-off, but Mama Neely did have her yearly chores: putting all the cold-weather clothes into boxes and storing them in the attic, changing the curtains, swapping out the bathroom décor with bright towels, rugs, and even new soap dishes.

As fate would have it, I married a woman with those same traits. So—what do we do for our spring cleaning? We *throw a party.* And you can't throw a party without good food. While Gina has the girls putting away winter clothes, changing linen, and bringing out the colors, I'm usually outside tuning up my grill. I know it won't be long before all of my girls show up on the patio for a break, after all their hard work, looking for some tasty grilled snacks.

GINA Okay, we all know that spring cleaning can be a pain in the you-know-what: tackling the closet, the linen, bringing out the new, and trying to figure out what you don't need. (Like that dress we finally realize we will never fit into . . .) But at the same time it is work that will lift your spirits (all those pretty bright colors). And you never know what you'll find. For example, we call my sister Kim the "quick knapper," because, whenever she visits and tries something on, the next thing we know it magically disappears. I was convinced she had a dress of mine, but during one spring cleaning session, I found that cute dress and had to call her and apologize!

But spring cleaning is not just about cleaning the house, it's also about cleaning the spirit. While you are throwing out the physical baggage, don't forget to throw out the emotional baggage as well. This menu is designed to make you feel good about letting go. So tape up that last box, put it in the attic (or on the porch, for Goodwill), have a tall glass of mint tea, and kick back. And if you missed a spot in the closet, not to worry—there's always next spring.

One-Handed Turkey Burgers

PAT Gina seasons these burgers perfectly. And unless you are standing in the kitchen while she's preparing them, you'll never be able to tell whether they're turkey or ground beef. Once these babies hit the grill and the sizzle starts, your neighbors will be peeking over the fence.

Ground turkey, as a rule, has less fat than ground beef, so don't buy lean ground turkey (also known as ground turkey breast). Instead, buy regular ground turkey, which is a mix of white and dark meat, and makes for a moister burger. We also add the garlic, shallot, cheddar cheese, and Worcestershire sauce to give it some extra juice and flavor. What you're left with is a healthy little handful (if you can eat just one!). **MAKES 12 MINI-BURGERS, SERVING 4**

2 cloves garlic, finely chopped

1 small shallot, finely chopped

½ cup grated cheddar cheese

1 pound ground turkey

Dash of Worcestershire sauce

Kosher salt and freshly ground black pepper

2 tablespoons olive oil, for brushing

12 small dinner rolls, split in half

2 plum tomatoes, sliced

Pickle slices, ketchup, mustard, or other condiments you like

Preheat your grill to medium heat, using charcoal, or heat a gas grill to medium-high heat.

Toss together the garlic, shallot, and cheese in a medium bowl. Mix in the ground turkey, Worcestershire sauce, salt, and pepper. Divide the burgers into twelve equal-sized patties (about 3 inches wide). Brush the patties with the olive oil.

Grill the burgers over medium heat for 4 or 5 minutes per side, or until cooked through.

Toast the rolls on the grill for the last few minutes of cooking the burgers. Lay the patties on the rolls, and top with sliced tomatoes and condiments of your choice.

Grilled Potato Wedges

We grill anything, and potatoes are no exception. The simplest way to grill sliced potatoes is to parboil them first. This makes for fast and even grilling. The calling card of these tasty taters is the appetizing grill marks that make them irresistible. That, and our house seasoning, when Neely's barbecue rub makes its annual spring debut. **SERVES 4 TO 6**

3 large russet potatoes, well scrubbed

Kosher salt and freshly ground black pepper

¼ cup olive oil

4 teaspoons Neely's barbecue rub (recipe follows)

Preheat the grill to medium heat.

Plop the potatoes into a large pot of cold salted water and bring to a boil. Reduce the heat, and simmer for 15 minutes, until the potatoes are just slightly tender but not cooked all the way through. Drain the potatoes, and dry well. Slice them into thick wedges, six wedges per potato.

Whisk together the olive oil, barbecue rub, salt, and pepper in a large bowl. Toss the potato wedges with the oil and seasoning. Grill the wedges, turning, for about 10 to 15 minutes, or until golden brown and crisp all over. Season with more salt and pepper before serving.

NOTE Be careful not to overboil your potatoes! Leaving some resistance in the boiled potatoes is a good idea; you don't want them to fall apart on the grill.

NEELY'S BARBECUE RUB

Remember to start with fresh spices for that sweet, savory, and spicy balance.

MAKES ABOUT 2½ CUPS

1½ cups paprika

¾ cup sugar

3¾ tablespoons onion powder

Stir together all the ingredients in a bowl. If stored in an airtight container in a cool, dry place, this seasoning will last for up to 6 months.

Chewy Pecan Bars

When you've got your hands full with cleaning, you don't have time for a full-on dessert stop. But these pecan bars will tempt you and "hit the spot," in addition to making an incredible snack-pack treat when you're on the go. Scrumptious brown sugar and chocolate are ooey, gooey, and satisfying, and they're the perfect reward for a day of hard work. **MAKES 36 SQUARES**

CRUST

2 cups all-purpose flour

1 teaspoon table salt

¼ teaspoon baking powder

½ cup (1 stick) butter, at room temperature

½ cup light-brown sugar

1 teaspoon pure vanilla extract

FILLING

1½ packed cups light-brown sugar

½ cup light corn syrup

2 tablespoons all-purpose flour

1 tablespoon bourbon

1 tablespoon pure vanilla extract

¾ teaspoon table salt

2 large eggs, lightly beaten

2 cups pecans, toasted, roughly chopped

1 cup mini–chocolate chips

Preheat the oven to 350 degrees F.

Line a 9-by-13-inch baking pan with foil, leaving 2 inches of overhang to use as handles to remove the bars at the end of baking.

Whisk together the flour, salt, and baking powder in a small bowl. Cream together the butter and light-brown sugar, using a hand mixer, in a separate, large bowl, until light and fluffy. Beat in the vanilla. Gradually pour in the dry mixture, and beat until the dough looks like coarse, pea-sized lumps. Use your hands to form the dough into a ball, then transfer it to your prepared baking pan and press down evenly to fill the pan. Bake for 20 minutes, or until lightly golden.

To make the filling: Combine the brown sugar, corn syrup, flour, bourbon, vanilla, salt, eggs, pecans, and chocolate chips in a large bowl. Remove the hot half-baked dough from the oven, and spread the filling over the crust. Return the pan to the oven, and bake for another 25 minutes, or until the top is puffed and brown and cracks begin to form (like a pecan-pie topping). Let cool for 45 minutes before slicing into squares.

Minted Iced Tea

This "house wine of the South" is literally drunk by the gallon during the spring and summer months here in Memphis. We add mint and simple syrup to ours, to give it the right amount of flavor and sweetness. It's a refreshing "knock-back," and can also be used as a mix for a cocktail (add a little rum or vodka). **SERVES 8**

12 cups water

10 bags tea (preferably Lipton)

1 bunch fresh mint, stems removed, leaves torn or bruised (save a few whole for garnish)

1 cup simple syrup (see below)

Lemons, for garnish

Bring the water to a simmer in a large pot. Remove the pot from the heat and add the tea bags and mint. Allow the tea and mint to steep for at least 10 minutes. Strain the steeped tea into a large glass pitcher, and allow to cool completely. Stir in the simple syrup.

Serve the tea over ice in a chilled Mason jar, with a sprig of mint and a lemon wheel for garnish.

SIMPLE SYRUP

Simple syrup is just that: simple and sweet. To make 1 cup, stir together (or shake in a bottle) 1 cup of water and 1 cup of sugar until dissolved. This one-to-one ratio ensures that your iced drinks stay cool and sweet. For a richer, sweeter version of simple syrup, you can do two parts sugar to one part boiling water, stirring just until dissolved, then setting aside to cool to room temperature. If you make up a batch, you can store it in your fridge in a well-sealed jar for up to 6 months.

Rehearsal Dinner

GINA   The night before the big day, brides are freaking out, wanting everything to be perfect . . . while grooms just want the rehearsal to be over so the real party can begin. Everybody is crazy, so I figured, why not make the dinner easy, light, and fun? You can do the froufrou stuff tomorrow, but tonight I'd want to be comfortable, spending the evening in my own skin, before the day I become Mrs. Him with all eyes on me.

In the South, we are big on catfish, and—sorry, ladies—we are *not* baking it. You just had your final fitting, so we are good to go with the fried food, and you simply can't have catfish without hush puppies and coleslaw. The peach spritzer is refreshing—let's not forget, *both* moms will be there, and we will need all the refreshing we can get. I also thought serving a "shot of love" was a great way to show everyone your appreciation for their sharing this special moment with you. Have the shot glass engraved with a special note, and send everyone on their way with a belly full of happiness and love to come . . . we all hope!

PAT'S PUNCH DRUNK IN LOVE

PAT   There is nothing like preparing and committing to spend the rest of your life with someone. The happiest day of my life was when Gina accepted my marriage proposal. (Hell, I still get goose bumps thinking about it, even though it's been over sixteen years since she accepted.)

I remember working all day, going home to shower, and racing down the highway to meet my sweetheart. I couldn't eat, sleep, work, walk, talk, or, yes, even *grill* without thinking about my *Gina*. So, when we decided that we wanted to spend the rest of our lives together, we moved on it fast. We didn't have the patience or the money to plan a wedding. This was our union, and we wanted it to be special. So we flew to Los Angeles, boarded a cruise ship, were married on deck, and then celebrated our honeymoon in Mexico.

It was an untraditional ceremony, and as much as our family wanted to be a part of the celebration, we were only thinking about how quick we could be Mr. and Mrs. We were "punch drunk in love." Now, of course, we dream of the day when Spenser and/or Shelbi will come in and announce, "I'm getting married." And if they decide to wed on a boat, it'd better be a big one, because we're

Shot of Love

These cute shot glasses fit the bill perfectly. You can buy them in bulk at your local restaurant-supply store, or online for a discounted price. Get them engraved, or make labels with your wedding date, or write a note and tie it to the glass with a decorative ribbon. Serve these with small demitasse spoons—because guests will want every last bit of that rich chocolate. When you think about it, special occasions don't come much bigger than this. So why not give them something to remember the occasion by? **MAKES 24 SHOTS OR EIGHT 6-OUNCE SERVINGS**

4 large egg yolks

¼ cup sugar

Pinch of salt

1 tablespoon bourbon

1 teaspoon pure vanilla extract

4 ounces bittersweet chocolate, finely chopped

4 ounces semisweet chocolate, finely chopped

2 cups heavy cream, chilled

Whipped cream and shaved chocolate, for garnish

Whisk together the egg yolks, sugar, salt, bourbon, and vanilla in a large glass bowl set over lightly simmering water (be sure the water is not touching the bottom of the bowl) until the sugar has dissolved and the egg mixture is warm, about 2 or 3 minutes.

Remove the mixture from the heat, and quickly whisk in the finely chopped chocolate until it's melted and completely smooth. Allow the chocolate mixture to cool to room temperature, about 5 minutes.

Whisk the heavy cream in another mixing bowl until soft peaks appear. Using a rubber spatula, gently fold the whipped cream into the chocolate mixture until no streaks of cream remain. Divide the mousse among twenty-four 2-ounce shot glasses (alternatively, you could use eight 6-ounce serving glasses). Chill the mousse for at least 2 hours before serving. When ready to serve, top with a small dollop of whipped cream and some shaved chocolate.

GINA'S TIP ON WHIPPED CREAM

I love making whipped cream, and I'm always looking for tips on how to make it easier. So I chill the bowl and beaters in the freezer before whipping. That way, my cream stays extra cold while it's whipping, and that speeds up the whole process.

May

MEMPHIS IN MAY

Sweet Cola BBQ Beef Ribs

Frozen Memphis Mint Juleps

Blueberry Pie

MOTHER'S DAY

Homemade Turkey Sausage Patties

Delightful Asparagus Frittata

Smoky Sweet Potato Cakes with Mama Callie's Maple Syrup

Mama's Day Off Cocktail

MEMORIAL DAY

Grilled Shrimp and Pineapple Skewers

Deluxe BBQ Burgers

Onion Rings

Neely's Coleslaw

Smoky Grilled Corn with Zesty Lime Butter

Classic Picnic Potato Salad

Easy Ice Cream Sandwiches

Berry Sangria

Memphis in May

PAT Talk about a time of year when this city comes alive, the people come together, and the smell of food alone will stop you in your tracks. For over twenty years, Memphians have gotten their party on for a solid month as part of the city's official Memphis in May celebrations. There are concerts, the symphony, barbecue competitions, and people from all over the country trying to figure out who is the best barbecuer in each category. It is a feast for all the senses.

Two of my favorite weekends are the music festival and the World Championship Barbecue Cooking Contest. The music fest is a large outdoor concert. Y'all know Gina loves to get her party on, and this is probably the weekend *she* loves most. There are food vendors up and down the blocked-off streets, and about a dozen musical acts per day for three or four days, with something for everyone, from rock to rap to R&B and even a little bit of country.

But the barbecue contest is my absolute favorite. Over 250 amateur teams from all over the country in a smokin' competition to be crowned champion. I originally loved this weekend because it was the busiest weekend of the year for Neely's Bar-B-Que, and I'm sure for all the other local barbecue restaurants as well. Customers line up out the door, hungry for a taste of true Memphis-style barbecue. We had only been in business a few years when the Memphis in May officials asked me to be a judge for the competition, which I did proudly for about eight years.

Things kick off on Friday night with an "Anything But" contest. This means anything but ribs, pork shoulder, and whole hog (the big three categories saved for Saturday's showdown). People are grilling and smoking everything but pork—from beef ribs and lamb to wild game or vegetables. I gained a lot of knowledge about what could possibly be grilled and smoked! Saturday morning is the Showdown. Judges show up bright and early at Tom Lee Park and are given a list of teams to judge. When I would arrive at a tent to judge a team, they'd usually be nervous as hell. These poor souls had prepared all year for the event; they normally started cooking the night before for ribs, and several days before if they were competing in the shoulder or whole-hog category. One thing I came to understand was that these people put their hearts and souls into the event, and the barbecue is always fantastic.

The last weekend of the month is usually the Sunset Symphony, which is a picnic-style event at Tom Lee Park, on the Mississippi. I call it a "recover party" after the month-long festivities. People bring blankets, picnic baskets, and their favorite bottles of wine. We watch the sun set and listen to one of the finest orchestras in the South, the Memphis Symphony. Even though I no longer judge in the MIM, May is still my favorite month here. Come visit then and you'll see why: you simply can't beat the flavor and the rhythm of Memphis.

NEELY'S RIBS GLORY

PAT In 1997, one of the local news stations decided that they wanted to stage a barbecue competition among the area restaurants. Mind you, local chefs and established restaurant owners *never* compete in the Memphis in May contest (because it's restricted to amateur cooking teams). So, when the news station called, we decided to submit our ribs. Can you believe we *won*? You know, all the big boys in Memphis were involved, and we had only been in business for a few years, so this was amazing. The local network sent an old 1950s fire engine over, and Tony and I were part of a huge parade downtown. Once we arrived at the river, we were given a torch to light the BBQ Bowl, which officially kicks off the weekend. It was a huge honor, and one of the proudest moments in our restaurant's history. The icing on the cake was that Al Roker came into town to present us with a trophy as the "Best BBQ in Memphis." This was too cool. I had never been on TV before, so of course I didn't sleep a wink the night before. Who would've thought that years later Gina and I would be hosting our own show?

Sweet Cola BBQ Beef Ribs

PAT Let me tell you, there's nothing like a perfectly seasoned smoked beef rib. Don't be intimidated by their size; beef ribs are easier to cook than pork ribs. Removing the silver membrane on the inside of the ribs is key, particularly with beef ribs that have thick skin. (Start at the end of the bone with your fingers and it'll pull right off.) Once the film of the membrane is removed, the sweet cherry-cola rub can really penetrate the meat. Cooking the ribs with indirect heat and hickory wood gives them a pull-off-the-bone tenderness and smoky flavor, and the sweet cherry-cola sauce added near the end infuses syrupy goodness into these beauties. **SERVES 4 TO 6**

SWEET CHERRY-COLA RUB

3 tablespoons light-brown sugar

3 tablespoons paprika

3 tablespoons kosher salt

2 tablespoons onion powder

1 tablespoon garlic powder

1 tablespoon freshly ground black
    pepper

2 slabs beef spare ribs (about
    8 pounds total)

2 cups sweet cherry-cola BBQ sauce
    (recipe follows)

To make the rub: Whisk together the first six ingredients in a small bowl. Reserve 1 tablespoon of the seasoning for the sauce that will finish the dish.

Rinse the ribs in cold water, then pat dry with paper towels, and pull off the thin silver membrane (see headnote). Season both sides of the slabs with the seasoning, and refrigerate for at least 12 hours.

Preheat the grill to 225 degrees F, preferably using hickory and charcoal. Place the slabs, meat side down, away from the flame, using indirect heat. Cook for 2 hours. Flip the slabs, and continue cooking for 45 minutes, or until you get the full bend in the slabs. Brush with the sweet cherry-cola BBQ sauce, and continue cooking for 15 minutes.

Remove from heat, slice into ribs, and serve with additional sauce.

SWEET CHERRY-COLA BBQ SAUCE

MAKES ABOUT 2 CUPS

1½ cups ketchup

One 12-ounce can cherry cola

¼ cup red-wine vinegar

¼ cup water

2 tablespoons light-brown sugar

2 tablespoons Worcestershire sauce

1 tablespoon sweet cherry-cola rub

Combine all ingredients in a large saucepan. Bring to a boil, then lower the heat and gently simmer for 1 hour, stirring occasionally.

COMEBACK SAUCE

MAKES SCANT ¾ CUP

This "secret sauce" can be made a day ahead—in fact, we recommend that you do that, to help those flavors marry well together. (It's called "Comeback Sauce" because they keep comin' back for more!)

¼ cup sour cream

2 tablespoons mayonnaise

2 tablespoons buttermilk

2 tablespoons Neely's BBQ sauce (see page 37)

Juice of ½ lemon

¼ teaspoon cayenne pepper

Kosher salt and freshly ground black pepper

Mix all the ingredients together in a small bowl. Let the sauce sit in the refrigerator as long as possible to let the flavors marry, or make the day ahead.

Onion Rings

One of the essential Southern side dishes is fried onion rings, and the key to great ones is the batter. Ours calls for buttermilk, cornmeal, hot sauce, and cayenne. The buttermilk and cornmeal will create a thick golden crust, and the hot sauce and the cayenne pepper give the rings a little kick.   **MAKES 6 SERVINGS**

Peanut oil, for deep-frying

2 cups buttermilk

1 tablespoon hot sauce, preferably Tabasco

1 egg, beaten

2 medium onions, sliced into ¾-inch-thick rings

1 cup all-purpose flour

1 cup yellow cornmeal

2 teaspoons seasoned salt

¼ teaspoon cayenne pepper

Kosher salt

Preheat the oil in a deep-fryer or Dutch oven to 375 degrees F. (For tips on deep-frying, see page 19.)

Whisk together the buttermilk, hot sauce, and egg in a large, wide dish. Slip in the onion slices, and allow them to soak for 5 minutes.

Toss the flour and cornmeal together in a large brown paper bag, and season with the seasoned salt and cayenne. Drop the onion rings into the paper bag in batches, and shake until they are covered.

Slip the onion rings into the oil, and fry until golden brown, about 2 minutes. Season with kosher salt as they come out of the fryer.

ALTERNATIVE
Baked Onion Rings

These are more tender than crisp, but that good onion flavor is still there.

Heat the oven to 425 degrees F. Spray two baking sheets with nonstick spray. Lay the battered rings out in a single layer on each sheet tray, and spray with the nonstick spray. Season with salt. Bake in the oven for 20 to 25 minutes, until golden.

Neely's Coleslaw

This is it: the famous sweet and spicy slaw from the restaurant that people come and buy by the bucketful. Make extra; trust us, you'll need it! **SERVES 6 TO 8**

1 small head green cabbage

1 small head red cabbage

4 carrots

1 medium yellow onion

½ cup mayonnaise

¼ cup prepared yellow mustard

2 teaspoons apple-cider vinegar

1 cup sugar

1 teaspoon freshly ground black pepper

½ teaspoon cayenne pepper

Kosher salt

Cut the cabbages into quarters, and remove the cores. Peel the carrots and onion, and slice them into pieces that will fit through the feed tube of a food processor. Fit the food processor with the large-holed grater attachment, and push the cabbage, carrots, and onion through the feed tube to grate. Pour the vegetables into a large bowl, and toss to combine.

Whisk together the mayonnaise, mustard, vinegar, sugar, black pepper, and cayenne in a medium bowl, whisking until the sugar is dissolved. Toss the coleslaw with the dressing, and season with salt and additional pepper to taste. Cover the slaw with plastic wrap, and chill for at least 2 hours before serving.

Smoky Grilled Corn with Zesty Lime Butter

There is nothing like grilled corn. Ours calls for butter spiked with lime, which gives it a citrus zing that acts as a perfect complement to smoky grilled corn. Rolling the husk back over the cob after adding the lime butter helps keep the corn from drying out. Some people prefer to soak the corn in a water bath beforehand, but this gives off steam when the corn is cooking inside the husk, and we prefer having the extra-smoky flavor instead. **SERVES 6**

6 ears corn

4 tablespoons butter, at room temperature

1 tablespoon fresh lime juice

½ teaspoon grated lime zest

Kosher salt and freshly ground black pepper

Preheat your grill to medium-high heat.

Pull the husk down from each cob and remove the fine silk.

Combine the butter, lime juice, zest, salt, and pepper in a medium bowl. Spread the butter all over the corn, and pull the husks back up.

Grill the corn, turning every few minutes, for 15 to 20 minutes, until the husk is charred. Peel back the husks to serve.

Classic Picnic Potato Salad

Everybody in the South has their own potato-salad recipe, and our version, using red potatoes and the coarse-ground, zippy Creole mustard, makes this a winner. Be sure to drain your potatoes thoroughly, because additional water will dilute the fantastic ingredients in the salad. It's best to dress the potatoes while they're still warm, so they can fully absorb the flavors. **SERVES 6 TO 8**

3 pounds red potatoes, scrubbed and cubed

Kosher salt and freshly ground black pepper

½ cup mayonnaise

¼ cup Creole mustard

1 tablespoon sugar

2 stalks celery, finely chopped

½ small red onion, finely chopped

2 tablespoons apple-cider vinegar

3 tablespoons roughly chopped fresh dill

1 teaspoon celery seed

2 hard-boiled eggs, chopped

Drop the potatoes into a large pot of cold salted water. Bring to a boil, then reduce the heat, and simmer for 15 minutes, or until the potatoes are tender. Drain the potatoes well in a colander.

Combine the mayonnaise, mustard, sugar, celery, red onion, apple-cider vinegar, dill, celery seed, and chopped eggs in a large bowl. Fold in the warm potatoes, and toss to combine. Cover the salad with plastic wrap, and refrigerate for at least 1 hour, or overnight for the best flavor.

Easy Ice Cream Sandwiches

PAT This is a simple and a delightful treat. Y'all know Gina loves pecans almost as much as she loves pigs. Well, maybe not that much. But butter-pecan ice cream—mmmm. Need I say more? **MAKES 6 SANDWICHES**

1 quart butter-pecan ice cream

Twelve 6-inch snickerdoodle cookies or any cookies of your choosing

1 cup chopped pecans

Let your ice cream sit out on the counter to soften for a good 10 to 15 minutes before you start building your sandwiches.

Lay six cookies top-side down. Scoop a generous helping of ice cream on each and, using a butter knife or off-set spatula, spread the ice cream to the edge of the cookie. Top with another cookie, and press together. Roll the sides of the sandwich into the chopped pecans. Place on a sheet tray, wrap in plastic wrap, and freeze the sandwiches for at least ½ hour before serving.

Berry Sangria

Ladies, this is my go-to drink on a warm summer day. And don't you know, men love it, too (even though it's pink!). It'll satisfy any thirst you may have worked up, but go easy, because even though it may taste like Hawaiian punch, it packs a wallop! **SERVES 6 TO 8**

1 bottle dry red wine

½ cup pineapple juice

½ cup strawberry nectar (found in the Latin-food section in grocery store)

¼ cup light rum

¼ cup Cointreau

1 cup raspberries

1 cup blueberries

Ice cubes

Mix all the ingredients except ice cubes together in a large pitcher. Refrigerate overnight, so all the flavors can marry, before serving in ice-filled glasses.

Graduation Day

PAT Gina and I graduated from Melrose High in Memphis. That's where we first fell in love. Boy, those were the days. I can remember graduation day like it was yesterday: Gina's maiden name was Ervin, so she walked the stage first, and I got to see this beautiful young woman receive her diploma. After the ceremony, our classmates were crying and saying how much they were going to miss everyone. (Three hundred–plus graduates! I know, right? Melrose was a very popular school.) I remember saying to myself, "Well, now, here comes the real work; playtime is over."

Gina and I spent graduation evening together at the house, where my mom had prepared a great dinner. Even though we had officially broken up (a high school reunion would bring us back together!), we were still good friends. This was probably our last dinner at the house before I went off to college and Gina moved to the West Coast. It was a process of out with the old and in with the new experiences, as I'm sure it was for Spenser and will be for Shelbi.

As a parent, graduation day can be one of the most emotional events in your lifetime. I know when Spenser walked across that stage to receive her diploma, my smile was so wide that my cheekbones were closing right in on my eyes. I had goose bumps, and it was hard to hold back the tears of joy. Her ceremony was in the evening, so we hosted a lunch at our home for family and friends the afternoon before the big event. (We knew that after graduating Spenser would want to hit the party circuit with her classmates.)

Here's the kicker: if you thought the graduation ceremony was emotional, try driving off campus and leaving your baby girl behind, because that's what comes next.

GINA Your kids' graduation day is always tough. How do you say goodbye to all those boo-boos you washed away? Impossible! Life is funny that way. You think you want your children gone, and find yourself saying, after a spat with them, "I'll be glad when you move out and see what life is *really* like." But then I think back to Pat's reaction when we took Spenser to college: I'm not sure he was ready to let go. Me? I wanted to see how my little bird would fly. Would the lessons and talks we'd had stick when I wasn't around? I felt deep in my heart that she had an angel looking over her, and I knew we had done our best as parents. Still, we didn't want her to forget about us, so we cooked and froze her favorite dishes and stuffed as many of them as we could in her mini-fridge. And then, after unpacking everything and waving goodbye, we cried all the way home.

Spicy Grilled Shrimp Cocktail

Oh my, if you love shrimp, this quick, easy grilled-seafood appetizer will make any celebration festive. **SERVES 6**

¼ cup olive oil

Juice and grated zest of 1 lemon

2 cloves garlic, minced

1 tablespoon finely chopped fresh thyme

1 tablespoon finely chopped fresh parsley

½ teaspoon crushed red-pepper flakes

Kosher salt and freshly ground black pepper to taste

2 pounds large shrimp, peeled and deveined

Twelve 8-inch wooden skewers, soaked in water for 30 minutes

Vegetable oil, for grilling

1 recipe chipotle cocktail sauce (recipe follows)

Green onions, for garnish (optional)

Preheat your grill to medium-high heat, using charcoal, or turn your gas grill to medium-high heat.

Whisk together the olive oil, lemon juice, lemon zest, garlic, herbs, red-pepper flakes, salt, and pepper in a casserole dish. Add the shrimp, and toss to coat. Thread the shrimp onto wooden skewers, four per skewer, being sure not to overcrowd them, so they can cook evenly. Let them marinate in the remaining sauce at room temperature for 15 minutes.

Lightly oil the grill grates with vegetable oil, using a clean tea towel. Grill the shrimp, 2 minutes per side. Remove the shrimp from the skewers, and place on a large platter. Sprinkle with green onions, and serve with the chipotle cocktail sauce.

CHIPOTLE COCKTAIL SAUCE

MAKES ABOUT 1 CUP

1 cup ketchup

1 tablespoon prepared horseradish

1 chipotle pepper packed in adobo sauce, minced

1 tablespoon adobo sauce

Juice of ½ lemon

Kosher salt and freshly ground black pepper

Combine all the ingredients in a medium bowl.

Mile-High Memphis BBQ Nachos

PAT These young graduates don't want a sit-down meal at their celebration. They want fun foods that they can eat (and spill all over your carpet!) while walking around and chatting with each other. Nachos fit the bill, and this Neely's Bar-B-Que version has been a signature dish in our restaurants for over 20 years. Smoked brisket, pulled pork, or store-bought rotisserie chicken—they all work just fine. And for you non–meat eaters, grilled vegetables work as well! **SERVES 6 TO 8**

One 16-ounce bag thick tortilla chips

1 pound processed American cheese, such as Velveeta, melted

1 cup Neely's BBQ sauce (page 37)

2 pounds easy BBQ pork (recipe follows, or store-bought)

One 4-ounce can sliced pickled jalapeños, drained

Preheat the oven to 400 degrees F.

Spread a single layer of tortilla chips out on a rimmed baking sheet. Drizzle with the cheese and BBQ sauce, and top with a few spoonfuls of pork or whatever meat you want to use. Make two more layers of chips, cheese, sauce, and meat. Bake until the cheese is bubbly and hot and the nachos are heated through, about 10 minutes. Garnish with the sliced pickled jalapeños.

NOTE If you decide to use rotisserie chicken for your meat in this recipe, it's easy to prepare. Just debone the chicken, remove the skin, and chop the meat in chunks on a cutting board. Wrap the meat in foil, and place it in a 350-degree oven to warm for a few minutes before adding it to the nachos.

Easy If-Ya-Ain't-Got-a-Smoker BBQ Pork

You don't always have to have an outside smoker, hickory smoke, charcoal, or even indirect heat to create delicious pulled pork. The secret lies in the smoked paprika and the fruit flavor from the apple juice; the lid should stay tight on your Dutch oven to keep in the tenderness. We don't need much of a dry rub for our pork, because the hot sauce, Worcestershire, and soy already make the Spice Fairy's presence known! **SERVES 4 TO 6**

One 2-pound chunk pork butt

Kosher salt and freshly cracked black pepper

1 tablespoon smoked paprika

½ cup Neely's BBQ sauce (see page 37)

½ cup apple juice

2 tablespoons apple-cider vinegar

1 dash of hot sauce, preferably Tabasco

1 dash of Worcestershire sauce

1 dash of soy sauce

Season the pork butt with salt, pepper, and the smoked paprika, and let rest in the refrigerator for at least 1 hour, or overnight.

Preheat your oven to 325 degrees F.

Place the pork butt in a small Dutch oven. Pour the BBQ sauce, apple juice, vinegar, hot sauce, Worcestershire, and soy sauce over the meat. Cover the pot with a secure lid, and put it in the oven. Cook until the pork is extremely tender, about 2½ hours. Remove the pot from the oven, and let the pork cool slightly before shredding.

Shred the meat in the Dutch oven, using two forks, so the meat can absorb more of the flavors of the cooking liquid. Let cool.

Neelys' If-You've-Got-a-Smoker BBQ Pork

If you've got a smoker or kettle grill, here's your recipe—you'll make much more pulled pork than you need for the nachos, but are you complaining? Ever heard of that Memphis classic, a pulled-pork sandwich? Make some Neely's coleslaw (see page 150), BBQ sauce (see page 37), and toasted hamburger buns, and go to town with the leftovers. **SERVES 12**

3 tablespoons Neely's barbecue rub (see page 112)

3 tablespoons coarsely ground black pepper

2 tablespoons kosher salt

One 10- to 12-pound pork shoulder or Boston butt

Mix together the Neely's barbecue rub, pepper, and salt.

Rinse the shoulder or butt thoroughly, pat dry with paper towels, and massage the seasoning mixture into the meat. Cover the meat with plastic wrap, and refrigerate for at least 2 hours, or up to 1 day in advance.

Following the manufacturer's instructions, and, using lump charcoal and ½ cup of soaked and drained wood chips for the smoker (or 1 cup for the kettle grill), start a fire, and bring the temperature of the smoker or barbecue grill up to 275 degrees F.

Place the pork on a rack in the smoker or on the grill. Cover, and cook the meat until a thermometer inserted into the center registers 165 degrees F, turning the pork every hour or so, about 6 hours total. Add more charcoal as needed to maintain the temperature, and more drained wood chips to maintain the smoke level.

Transfer the pork to a rimmed baking sheet (this is important—you'll want to catch all the flavorful juices), and allow it to stand until cool enough to handle. Shred the pork into bite-sized pieces, and mound on a platter. Pour any juices from the baking sheet over the pork. At this point the pork can be served immediately, or covered with foil and refrigerated for a day.

If you chill the pork, rewarm it, covered, in a 350-degree oven for about 30 minutes.

Big Green Salad with Cherry Tomatoes and Buttermilk Dressing

This dressing is so easy and flavorful, with lots of tang as well as creaminess. Dress your greens just before serving, to avoid that limp and soggy salad sadness.

SERVES 4 TO 6

DRESSING

1 clove garlic, finely chopped

1 teaspoon apple-cider vinegar

1 tablespoon honey

Juice of 1 lemon

⅓ cup buttermilk, well shaken

3 tablespoons mayonnaise

2 tablespoons chopped fresh
   parsley

Kosher salt and freshly ground
   black pepper

2 large heads butter lettuce,
   leaves torn

2 cups cherry tomatoes, halved

Whisk together the garlic, apple-cider vinegar, honey, lemon juice, buttermilk, mayonnaise, parsley, salt, and pepper in a small bowl. If you have time, cover the bowl with plastic wrap and chill in the fridge for 1 hour before serving.

Put the lettuce and cherry tomatoes in a large serving bowl. Toss with the dressing, and season with salt and pepper. Serve immediately.

Grilled Mini-Pizzas: Roasted Vegetable with Smoked Mozzarella, and Pepperoni and Jalapeño

Don't let these puppies fool you. We call them mini-pizzas, but there's nothing all that little about them, in either size or flavor. It just makes us feel better, because you find yourself eating a lot of them before you know it! **SERVES 4 TO 6**

PIZZA SAUCE

1 tablespoon olive oil

3 cloves garlic, chopped

½ teaspoon crushed red-pepper flakes

One 32-ounce can crushed tomatoes

¼ cup torn fresh basil leaves

Kosher salt and freshly ground black pepper

Pinch of sugar (optional)

ROASTED VEGETABLE WITH SMOKED MOZZARELLA PIZZA TOPPINGS

1 cup cherry tomatoes, halved

1 red bell pepper, seeded, cut into 1-inch chunks

1 small zucchini, quartered, cut into chunks

1 small red onion, sliced into ½-inch-thick rings

3 tablespoons olive oil, plus more for the grill and dough

Kosher salt and freshly ground black pepper

12 ounces smoked mozzarella cheese, grated

¼ cup torn fresh basil leaves

Make the pizza sauce: Heat the olive oil in a medium sauté pan until hot. Toss in the garlic and red-pepper flakes, and cook, stirring, until the garlic is fragrant and golden, about 1 minute. Lower heat, add the tomatoes, and let simmer for 10 minutes. Stir in the basil, and season with salt and pepper. Taste for seasoning. If the sauce needs some sweetening (it will depend on the tomatoes you are using), add a pinch of sugar.

Prepare the roasted vegetable pizza toppings: Preheat the oven to 450 degrees F. Toss the tomatoes, red pepper, zucchini, red onion, and olive oil together on a rimmed baking sheet, seasoning with salt and pepper. Roast until the veggies are tender, about 20 minutes, and set aside.

Preheat the grill to medium heat. Make sure the grill grate is very clean by scrubbing it with a grill brush. Carefully (and quickly) oil the grate with olive oil, using a crumpled-up paper towel.

Cut each dough ball in half. Flour your work surface, and gently stretch two of the dough halves out to 8-inch rounds. Gently place the stretched dough on the grill grates over indirect heat, well clear of any direct flame, and cover with lid. Let the dough cook for 2 or 3 minutes, until the crust starts to become crisp and browned. (It's a good idea to take a peek to make sure the underside of the dough is not getting too dark. If it is, pull it even farther away from the heat.) If all is well and the dough is looking good, brush the top side of the dough with olive oil and carefully flip, using a pair of tongs, keeping the pizza crust on the cooler area of the grill, well away from direct heat.

Spread a nice ladleful of sauce on each of the grilled pizza-dough rounds. For the veggie pizza, first top a round with half of the smoked

Two 1-pound balls pizza dough, store-bought or homemade, at room temperature

PEPPERONI AND JALAPEÑO PIZZA TOPPINGS

8 ounces part-skim mozzarella cheese, grated (about 2 cups)

4 ounces pepperoni, sliced

1 jalapeño, thinly sliced

mozzarella and then half of the roasted vegetables. For the pepperoni pizza, first top the other dough round with half of the plain mozzarella, then half of the pepperoni and half of the sliced jalapeño.

Cover the grill with the lid, and cook for another 2 or 3 minutes, until the cheese is melted and bubbly and the crusts are crisp. Remove the pizzas from the heat.

Top the veggie pizza with fresh basil, then cut both pizzas into slices and serve. Repeat with the other halves of the dough balls and toppings.

NOTE Get everything in place by your grill before you start working, because grilled pizza cooks fast, and any delay may char that crust.

Creamsicle Float

PAT Now, y'all know I'm crazy about my ice cream, so sometimes I disregard the set quantities in this recipe and put in ten scoops. Sorry, I just can't help myself. Gina says I got a real problem. The first step is to admit you have a problem, so here it is. "Hello, my name is Pat, and I'm an ice-cream-aholic."

GINA To make this PG drink a little more R-rated, add a shot of orange-flavored liquor (such as Absolut Mandarin) or vanilla-flavored vodka to the juice.

MAKES 4 FLOATS

8 scoops vanilla ice cream

One 16-ounce can frozen orange-juice concentrate

2 cups cream soda, chilled

Fresh whipped cream

Orange zest, grated, for garnish

Place two scoops of ice cream in each of four frosty pint glasses. Divide the orange concentrate between the glasses, and top each with ½ cup cream soda, stirring to combine. Finish the floats with a nice dollop of whipped cream and a sprinkling of orange zest.

Father's Day Barbecue

PAT This is my day, but it wasn't until Gina and I were married and I became a proud father that I realized how special the day was. See, you've got to remember that I lost my father and both grandfathers before I was thirteen. My father would have spoiled Spenser and Shelbi rotten—man, he loved little girls. I remember my sister, Jackie, getting away with murder! We couldn't look at her wrong, because if she told Daddy the blame was on us!

I guess, the older I get, the more I miss him. I would talk to him about marriage and raising kids if I could, and I would love to take him fishing or to play golf. How cool would it be to have him on *Down Home with the Neelys*, grillin' with me? He also loved to dance, and I can see how he'd have cut a rug with Gina. On Father's Day in particular, I am very conscious that he is watching me all the time. Here's to you, Daddy!

These days, Gina and I travel so much that we'll sometimes miss a holiday, something neither of us likes to do. Recently, Gina and I were traveling on Father's Day, and it was one of the worst days of my life. When we left in the morning, the girls were standing in the driveway watching the car pull away. I had dark shades on so that they couldn't see my eyes, but at moments like this, you can't hold back the tears.

Gina, Spenser, and Shelbi treat me like a king on Father's Day. The two most frequently asked questions: "Daddy, can we get you anything?" and "What would you like for dinner?" The truth is, what's meaningful to me on Father's Day is spending time with my three beautiful girls.

This Father's Day menu features all my favorites: bone-in rib-eye steak and potatoes, along with ice cream (y'all knew that was coming). All you dads on Father's Day, surround yourself with your children, invite your own father over, make sure your significant other is by your side, and eat well.

GINA If I know one thing about my man, it's that he loves meat, potatoes, something sweet, and *me!* I hope not in that order. . . . He loves a big fat char-grilled rib eye, but the bone has to be in it, because it adds more flavor, and I like to serve his with a dab of herb butter to complement the meat. His other favorite is fingerling potatoes, because they look like his hands (I know, he's a strange man), so I give those a good smash and add all the seasonings. Now, here's the sneaky part: he likes strawberry ice cream with shortbread, but it is my absolute favorite as well, so I get to have a bite. . . . Sneaky, right?

HAPPY DADDY DAY
TO ALL THE GREAT DADS.

We really do appreciate you.

Spicy Grilled Cheese Bread

PAT I refer to this dish as "sophisticated cheese toast." Gina and I actually got the idea from a famous Memphis restaurant, though in our version we make it with baguettes, because we are going to grill these puppies, and baguettes can withstand the heat. Now, you can use any cheese you like, but on my spicy grilled cheese bread, we must have Parmesan and mozzarella. **SERVES 6 TO 8**

3 tablespoons olive oil

2 cloves garlic, minced

1/2 teaspoon crushed red-pepper flakes, or more to taste

Kosher salt and freshly ground black pepper

8 slices baguette, sliced 1/2 inch thick on the diagonal

1/4 cup grated Parmesan cheese

1/4 cup grated mozzarella cheese

Preheat the grill to medium-high heat.

Combine the olive oil, garlic, red-pepper flakes, salt, and pepper in a ramekin. Brush both sides of the bread with the oil. Grill the bread on each side for 2 or 3 minutes, until nice grill marks appear. For the final minute of grilling, evenly top the bread slices with both cheeses, and close the grill so the cheese will melt. Remove the baguette slices from the grill to a platter.

Char-Grilled Rib Eye with Roasted Shallot and Herb Butter

There is nothing like a rib eye: it is the most flavorful steak you can buy. The thin streams of fat running through this cut of steak create *outstanding* flavor. You'll only need to season this with salt and pepper, because we're going to make a shallot-and-herb butter to slap on top of this baby once it's off the grill. As with any good steak, let this one rest for a few minutes before digging in. It will be moist and tender. **SERVES 4 GENEROUSLY**

Four 12-ounce rib-eye steaks, bone-in, about 1½ inches thick

Olive oil

Kosher salt and freshly ground black pepper

1 recipe roasted shallot and herb butter (recipe follows)

Take your steaks out of the fridge 30 minutes before you want to start grilling, so they can come to room temperature.

Prepare the charcoal grill to medium-high heat on one side of your grill, and medium-low heat on the other. You will need just a few briquettes on the cooler side of the grill to maintain the low heat. (If using a gas grill, heat one side of the grill to medium-high heat and the other to low.)

When the grill is hot and ready to go, brush the grill grates with some olive oil. Season the steaks generously with salt and pepper. Place the steaks on the hot side of the grill for 3 to 4 minutes, then flip and grill for another 4 minutes. Once the steaks have a nice caramelized crust, move them to the cooler part of the grill, and continue cooking for 6 to 7 minutes for medium rare, or 8 to 9 minutes for medium.

Remove the steaks from grill, and tent loosely with foil to keep warm. Let the steaks rest for 5 minutes, so the juices can redistribute throughout the meat.

Spread the steaks with the roasted shallot and herb butter.

NOTE When you're grilling such a thick piece of meat, it's best to cook at a high temperature, to sear the outside nicely, then move to the cooler side of the grill, to give the inside of the steak a moment to catch up. This is especially important if you like your steaks the way Pat does, more on the medium side than medium rare.

ROASTED SHALLOT AND HERB BUTTER

GINA Roasting the shallot gives it a deep, sweet flavor, and the lemon zest lightens the whole thing up. This butter would also be an excellent topping for fish or chicken.

1 medium shallot, peeled

1 tablespoon olive oil

Kosher salt and freshly ground
    black pepper

1 stick salted butter, at room
    temperature

1 tablespoon finely chopped fresh
    parsley

1 tablespoon finely chopped fresh
    basil

1 tablespoon finely chopped fresh
    tarragon

1 teaspoon grated lemon zest

Pinch of crushed red-pepper flakes

Preheat the oven to 350 degrees F.

Place the shallot on a square of foil, drizzle lightly with olive oil, and season with salt and pepper. Fold up the foil into a little packet, and place in the oven for 1 hour. Let cool completely.

Pulse the roasted shallot and remaining ingredients in a food processor until combined but still coarse. Scrape the butter onto a piece of plastic wrap, spread it across lengthwise, and roll into a log. Twist the ends to seal. Place in the fridge to firm up for at least 35 minutes before serving.

Smashed Fingerling Potatoes

PAT I told y'all, I can't have steak without potatoes, and fingerling potatoes are my choice. These rich and creamy little darlings are about the size of my fingers, and they are firm enough to withstand the heat of my grill. A great tip for grilling potatoes is to boil them a bit first; this will give you faster and more even grilling. The olive oil will keep them moist and let the rosemary and garlic do their aromatic thing. **SERVES 6**

2 pounds fingerling potatoes, scrubbed well

Kosher salt

Olive oil, to coat

2 cloves garlic, minced

2 tablespoons chopped fresh rosemary leaves

Freshly ground black pepper to taste

Slip the potatoes into a large pot of cold water, and bring to a boil. Add a few large pinches of salt, and simmer until just tender, about 10 minutes. Drain, and let cool for about 20 minutes.

Once the potatoes are cool enough to handle, place them on a sheet tray and gently press them down to flatten. (It helps to use the edge of a large clean chef's knife, pressing the potatoes down flat one at a time, until they flatten to a 1½-inch thickness.) Drizzle on the olive oil, and add the garlic, rosemary, salt, and pepper. Gently toss until the potatoes are well coated.

Heat your grill to medium heat. Remove the potatoes from the sheet tray, and grill them until they are golden brown and crisp, about 4 or 5 minutes per side.

Remove the crispy potatoes to a platter. Give them a taste, and add more salt and freshly ground black pepper if necessary.

NOTE The trick here is to not overboil your potatoes. You don't want the potatoes to crumble and fall through your grill grates!

Fresh Strawberry Ice Cream with Shortbread Crumble

PAT I guess you could say I developed a love of ice cream because of my grandmother. For her, only homemade would do, and her homemade was some of the very best. Her fresh strawberry ice cream was one of my favorites. It so happens that Father's Day falls smack in the middle of strawberry season—and don't you know it, Grandma, I'm taking a page from your playbook. There's something about fresh strawberries and cream, and when you spoon out a mouthful of this ice cream, you'll see what I mean. The best thing about this recipe is that you can make more and have some for *the day after* Father's Day. The sweetened condensed milk makes this a creamy, very soft, and scoopable ice cream. **MAKES 1 QUART**

2 pints fresh strawberries, hulled, roughly chopped

¼ cup sugar

14 ounces sweetened condensed milk

1½ cups heavy cream

1 teaspoon pure vanilla extract

Crumbled shortbread cookies (preferably Lorna Doone)

Fresh whipped cream, for serving

Freeze the ice-cream-maker bowl for a full 24 hours before making the ice cream.

Toss the strawberries and sugar in a large bowl, and let it sit at room temperature for 15 minutes, so the berries can macerate and the sugar can dissolve. Drain the berries of any liquid, then mash the fruit well with a wooden spoon until the strawberries are juicy with some small chunks.

Mix the condensed milk, cream, and vanilla together in a large measuring cup, stir in the strawberry mixture, and chill at least 1 hour, or as long as overnight.

Pour the mixture into your chilled ice-cream-maker bowl, and churn until it freezes to a soft frozen state, about 15 to 25 minutes (depending on your machine). Put the bowl with the ice cream in the freezer to continue firming up for another 3 hours.

Sprinkle some crumbled shortbread cookies on top of each serving, and top with a nice dollop of whipped cream.

July

FOURTH OF JULY

Bourbon BBQ Glazed Ribs

Honey BBQ Sticky Drumsticks

Summer Rice Salad

Mama Neely's Baked Beans

Grilled Apricot and Peach Shortcake

Watermelon Cooler

SWEET TEA AND SYMPATHY

Chicken and Biscuits

Marinated Broccoli Salad

Whipped Garlicky Mashed Potatoes (see page 67)

Lemon Squares

Minted Iced Tea (see page 114)

Fourth of July

PAT When I was a child, the charcoal and hickory from the smoke-filled back-yards in my neighborhood gave off an aroma for blocks and blocks. On the Fourth in my house, there were always ribs, baked beans, watermelon, and delicious desserts, and my brother Tony always wanted to make the barbecue sauce. He loved taking a generic sauce and adding lemon juice, spices, and other things he wouldn't even mention to us to make it his own, and, you know what, it always turned out pretty good. So, of course, when we opened Neely's Bar-B-Que, Tony became our "sauce man."

The Fourth is one of our biggest celebrations of the year. In the days leading up to it, family and friends will start calling and asking, "What time will the ribs be ready, and what can I bring?" We always tell them, "Bring your appetite, because we're going to be doing some serious eating over here!"

GINA Growing up, we always got dressed up in red, white, and blue outfits for the Fourth. My mom didn't allow fireworks, but she would bend on the spar-klers. (I remember thinking how pretty they looked, which may explain why I like to "sparkle" today.) Neighbors would start cooking their ribs the day before and tend to them all night, to make sure they came out just right. This was the "brag-ging" holiday, one that separated the men from the boys. And you know what it all came down to? *Those ribs.* Whose were the most tender? Whose had the most flavor? Whose featured the best sauce? The guys would go at it as if they were in competition. My great-great-grandmother Mama Callie would light a fire for the grill out back, while my mom would make a potato salad that no one could touch—and she still does. Kim, Tanya, and Jackie would bake everything else, and I was the little "runner," always in the way, listening to lively conversation (or gossip), and waiting on them to cut that watermelon. If I complained too long, my sisters would give me a freeze pop to shut me up. One of our cardinal rules on the Fourth: you got to have watermelon. You can eat it as is, or have a watermelon cooler like the one we feature in this chapter. Either way, you're getting it.

Sparklers, fireworks, and watermelon! That's just about as perfect as it gets.

Bourbon BBQ Glazed Ribs

PAT My brothers and I are all "bourbon men." We take ours neat, or lacquered to our ribs. Enough said.

GINA I can't believe I ended up with a bourbon-and-ribs man. Growing up, we always had chicken, hot dogs, smoked sausages, and burgers, but for some reason the *ribs* were always center stage. The women in my family were often throwing some crazy ingredient or other into their rubs and sauces—and don't you know that we kept bourbon as one of them. We always had bourbon around for "ailments," and not just the cooking kind.

So what do I do? I go and marry a rib-grilling bourbon lover—was my life being planned even then? To this day, ribs and bourbon are like the "main act" in my life! Remember: in all grilling, the sauce and the rub must work together, like a good marriage. And when smoking those ribs, Pat will remind you to keep the heat "low and slow." **SERVES 4 TO 6 AS AN APPETIZER**

RUB

¼ **cup kosher salt**

3 **tablespoons light-brown sugar**

1 **tablespoon garlic powder**

1 **tablespoon onion powder**

1 **tablespoon ground cumin**

1 **tablespoon chile powder**

2 **teaspoons freshly ground black pepper**

1 **teaspoon cayenne pepper**

Two 3-pound slabs pork spare ribs, untrimmed

Combine all of the rub ingredients in a small bowl.

Rinse off the ribs in cold water to get rid of any impurities, and pat dry. Place the ribs, curled side up, on a flat work surface, and remove the silver membrane that lines the bones. This will allow the flavors of the rub to permeate the meat fully and make the ribs very tender. Trim the ribs to remove the extra fat. Place them in a rimmed dish, and season on all sides with the rub. Cover the dish with plastic wrap, and place in the fridge for 8 hours or overnight.

Start on your sauce: Pour the canola oil into a large saucepan set over medium heat. Once it's hot, toss in the onion and garlic, and sauté until tender, about 4 minutes. Stir in the ketchup, bourbon, vinegar, brown sugar, molasses, Worcestershire, hot sauce, paprika, and mustard powder. Bring to a simmer, and cook, stirring occasionally, for 30 minutes, until the mixture is thick and coats the back of a spoon. Season with salt and pepper.

When you're ready to cook the ribs, preheat your grill to 250 degrees F, using a combination of charcoal and hickory. When coals are ready, mound them to one side to create indirect heat.

(continued)

SAUCE

1 tablespoon canola oil

1 small onion, finely chopped

2 cloves garlic, finely chopped

2 cups ketchup

½ cup bourbon

¼ cup apple-cider vinegar

¼ cup light-brown sugar

3 tablespoons mild molasses

1 tablespoon Worcestershire sauce

1 tablespoon hot sauce, preferably Tabasco

2 teaspoons paprika

1 teaspoon mustard powder

Kosher salt and freshly ground black pepper to taste

Place the slabs on the grill, curled side up, spacing them to be as far away from the direct flame as possible. Cook the ribs, covered, for 2 hours. Flip the slabs over to finish cooking, and cover and cook for another ½ hour. Once you see a full bend in the ribs, brush the barbecue sauce all over them, cover with the lid, and let cook for another 10 minutes.

Pull the ribs from the grill, and slice between the bones into individual portions. Serve with the extra sauce on the side.

NOTE If you've got a grill that's on the larger side, go ahead and throw on a third slab. There's enough rub and sauce here to go around.

Honey BBQ Sticky Drumsticks

PAT When hosting on a day as important to everybody as the Fourth of July, you've got to have some chicken on the menu for the non-pork eaters. (We will never understand how you could be a non-porker, but that's for another book.)

GINA I've always loved drumsticks for their juicy dark meat, and the way they would fit so neatly in my hand when my sister Kim used to fry them for me. Now Shelbi loves drumsticks, too!

The combination of honey, orange, and ancho-chile powder, with just the right amount of heat, and the smoke of a grill—baby, these drumsticks are so good they'll make you want to smack your mama or the cook (although I wouldn't recommend it!). Allowing the drumsticks to marinate overnight, and then "mopping" on the glaze at the end, will ensure your guests' memberships in the clean-plate club. **SERVES 6**

ORANGE RUB

2 teaspoons freshly grated orange zest

1 teaspoon ancho-chile powder

1½ teaspoons kosher salt

1 teaspoon smoked paprika

½ teaspoon freshly ground black pepper

12 chicken drumsticks (about 3 pounds)

HONEY ORANGE GLAZE

4 tablespoons butter

¼ cup honey

¼ cup freshly squeezed orange juice

1 tablespoon Dijon mustard

For the rub: Whisk together orange zest, chile powder, salt, smoked paprika, and black pepper in a small bowl. Season the outside of the chicken drumsticks with the rub, then carefully loosen the skin with your index finger and season the meat underneath. Place the drumsticks in a dish, cover with plastic wrap, and let marinate for at least 1 hour or overnight in the refrigerator.

For the glaze: Melt the butter in a small saucepan set over medium heat. Stir in the honey, orange juice, and Dijon mustard, and simmer for 1 minute. Remove from heat.

Preheat your grill to medium heat. Brush the grill grates with olive oil to keep the chicken from sticking.

Grill the drumsticks, turning frequently, until they're cooked through and the skin is crisp, about 25 to 35 minutes. Brush with the glaze, and grill 5 more minutes.

Summer Rice Salad

PAT Grilled corn is good enough all by itself. Here we feature it in a light, slightly smoky salad with rice, bell peppers, cherry tomatoes, and kidney beans. It's an awesome combination, but once you add in the feta cheese, "Girl, you *did* that!" That's what Gina's mom always says. We used white rice, but brown will work just as well and give it an earthy, nutty flavor. **SERVES 6**

2 ears corn, husked

3 tablespoons olive oil, plus more for brushing corn

Kosher salt and freshly ground black pepper to taste

1½ cups cooked long-grain white rice

1 red bell pepper, chopped

1 cup cherry tomatoes, halved

One 15.5-ounce can kidney beans, drained and rinsed

4 green onions, sliced

Juice of 1 lemon

1 teaspoon ground cumin

1 clove garlic, finely chopped

2 tablespoons chopped fresh parsley

1 tablespoon finely chopped fresh mint

⅔ cup crumbled feta cheese

Preheat the grill to medium-high heat.

Brush the corn with olive oil, and sprinkle with salt and pepper. Grill for 5 to 6 minutes, rotating on all sides, until the corn has some nice charred spots. Let cool, and use a sharp knife to strip the corn kernels from the cob and into a large bowl. Add the rice, red bell pepper, tomatoes, beans, and green onions, tossing to mix.

Whisk together the olive oil, lemon juice, cumin, garlic, parsley, mint, salt, and pepper in a smaller bowl. Fold the dressing into the vegetables, and top with the crumbled cheese.

Toss well.

Mama Neely's Baked Beans

PAT Every Fourth of July, Mama Neely made her famous baked beans: she'd brown ground beef and then doctor that beef with molasses, brown sugar, and plenty of spices. Let me tell you, those beans were good. And so are these. We've found that using smoked sausage in place of the ground beef (or pork shoulder, as in our restaurant recipe) adds a smoky depth to the dish. Once you make these beans, there is no going back. If you want to put your own spin on it, you can use kidney beans instead of pork and beans, but I say my mama's way is best. **SERVES 6**

2 tablespoons canola oil

1 large onion, finely chopped

3 cloves garlic, finely chopped

½ pound smoked sausage, sliced

Three 16-ounce cans pork and beans

½ cup ketchup

½ cup light molasses

¼ cup light-brown sugar

2 tablespoons apple-cider vinegar

2 tablespoons prepared mustard

Dash of hot sauce, preferably Tabasco

Preheat the oven to 350 degrees F.

Heat the oil in a Dutch oven set over medium-high heat. Once it's hot, toss in the onion and garlic, and sauté until the onion is tender, about 3 or 4 minutes. Add the sausage, and continue to cook until the meat has browned, about 4 minutes more. Stir in the pork and beans, ketchup, molasses, sugar, vinegar, mustard, and hot sauce. Bring the beans up to a simmer, then put in the hot oven for 45 minutes, uncovered, until the mixture is bubbly and thick.

Chicken and Biscuits

We like to refer to this dish as our sophisticated chicken potpie. Lord knows we love chicken, and when you add the sweetness of Vidalia onion, carrots, and celery, you are on your way to some classic Southern comfort food. And we all need a little bit of that sometimes, don't we? **SERVES 6**

CHICKEN FILLING

½ cup (1 stick) butter, plus more for greasing

4 cups chicken broth

1 Vidalia onion, chopped

2 large carrots, sliced into ¼-inch-thick half-moons

2 stalks celery, chopped

3 cloves garlic, chopped

Kosher salt and freshly ground black pepper to taste

½ cup all-purpose flour

¾ cup heavy cream

1 cup frozen peas

4 cups shredded cooked chicken (from 3-pound rotisserie chicken)

¼ cup sliced green onions

BISCUIT TOPPING

2 cups all-purpose flour

2 teaspoons baking powder

1 teaspoon baking soda

1 teaspoon kosher salt

6 tablespoons cold butter, cut into ½-inch cubes

1½ cups buttermilk

2 tablespoons melted butter

2 tablespoons finely grated Parmesan cheese

Preheat your oven to 375 degrees F. Butter a 3-quart casserole dish.

For the filling: Pour the chicken broth into a large saucepan. Heat until warm. Set aside.

Melt the butter in a large high-sided skillet set over medium heat. Add the onion, carrots, celery, and garlic, and sauté until tender and the onion is translucent, about 8 minutes. Season to taste with salt and pepper. Sprinkle in the flour, and stir with a wooden spoon until the moistened flour becomes light blond in color, about 2 minutes. Stir in the hot broth and the heavy cream. Bring the liquid to a boil, then reduce the heat so it reaches a simmer. Stir in the peas, chicken, and green onions. Pour the whole mixture into the buttered casserole dish.

For the biscuit topping: Whisk together the flour, baking powder, baking soda, and salt. Cut the butter cubes into the flour, using your fingers, until the mixture looks like little peas. Stir in the buttermilk until just combined.

Drop the biscuit batter in large lumps on top of the chicken mixture, covering the surface evenly. Drizzle the melted butter over the tops of the biscuits, then sprinkle with the Parmesan. Bake for 30 to 35 minutes, uncovered, or until the biscuit crust is golden brown and the filling is bubbly.

Marinated Broccoli Salad

PAT Broccoli, broccoli, broccoli! We *love* this simple vegetable. Nothing is easier than blanching broccoli, and once this delicious dressing—a little sweet, a little savory, a little sour, and a little spicy—is added, the transportable dish becomes super-duper. As Gina always says, "A great dressing is like a great handbag and shoes. It makes the whole outfit look (taste) perfect." **SERVES 4 TO 6**

Kosher salt

6 cups broccoli florets

2 tablespoons honey

3 tablespoons red-wine vinegar

1 teaspoon crushed red-pepper flakes

Freshly ground black pepper

⅓ cup extra-virgin olive oil

6 slices bacon, cooked, crumbled

½ small red onion, chopped

½ cup slivered almonds, toasted

½ cup dried cranberries

Prepare a large pot of boiling salted water and a large bowl of ice water. Blanch the broccoli in the boiling water until tender-crisp and bright green, about 1 minute. Drop the broccoli immediately into the ice water to stop the cooking. Drain, and dry well.

Whisk together the honey, vinegar, red-pepper flakes, salt, and pepper in a large bowl. Slowly add the olive oil, whisking to emulsify. Add the broccoli, bacon, red onion, almonds, and cranberries, and toss well to combine. Cover with plastic wrap and let the salad marinate and chill for 2 hours before serving.

Lemon Squares

GINA There's something about the smell and taste of fresh lemon that livens a dish right up. I remember my great-great-grandmother always rolled lemons on the counter before slicing them, to get the full flavor and extract all the juices, so I do it, too. I'm having a moment just thinking about watching her. Lemon squares are easy to prepare, and give you an Old South flavor that takes you right back in time. And the confectioners' sugar at the end doesn't hurt one bit. **MAKES 24 SQUARES**

CRUST

½ cup cold butter, diced

1 cup all-purpose flour

¼ cup confectioners' sugar, plus
    more for dusting

Dash of salt

1 egg yolk, chilled

2 tablespoons ice water

LEMON FILLING

4 large eggs

1¼ cups granulated sugar

1 tablespoon all-purpose flour

1 teaspoon baking powder

Juice of 3 lemons

Zest of 1 lemon, grated

Preheat the oven to 325 degrees F and adjust rack to center.

Put the butter, flour, confectioners' sugar, and salt in a food processor, and pulse in short intervals until the mixture is crumbly and resembles small peas. Add the cold egg yolk and water to the mixture, and pulse until just mixed. Place the dough on a floured surface, knead just a few times, and form into a disk. Wrap in plastic, and keep in the refrigerator until cold, about 30 minutes.

When the dough is cold, roll it out on the floured work surface, and cover the bottom of a 9-by-13-inch pan with it. Bake for 20 minutes, or until lightly golden. Remove, and let cool slightly.

Whisk together the eggs, sugar, flour, baking powder, lemon juice, and zest in a bowl. Pour the filling over the hot crust.

Bake for 30 minutes, until the lemon center sets. Remove from the oven, cool completely, dust with confectioners' sugar, and cut into squares.

August

GIRLS' NIGHT

Chicken Pot Stickers

Fig and Arugula Flatbread

Flower Power

MINI-MOON

Grilled Bacon-Wrapped Shrimp
with Sweet and Spicy Orange Dipping Sauce

Green Herb Salad with Roasted Red Pepper Feta Dressing

Grilled Lobsters with Lemon Basil Butter

Poached Peaches and Cream

Girls' Night

GINA Yippee! It's Girls' Night! Take down the ponytails, loosen the weaves, unbutton those top buttons, and take off the damn girdles!

Every now and then, life calls for a night when we can regroup or refuel. No, scratch that—we need to regroup and refuel *as often as we can.* We ladies wear so many hats, and want to satisfy so many people, that we forget about satisfying our own sweet selves. So I like to make this night as special as possible. Three or four of my friends and I take turns hosting, usually on a Friday night, starting at five, for a few hours. Once, I even hired a masseuse to relieve all the extra tensions. Ladies, those feet have special pressure points—treat them right.

Because I generally bite off too much, I always enlist Pat to help me create a very simple menu. (Admittedly, it's all about the cocktails and talk anyway, but we need food for stamina.) Once things are set, Pat usually runs out of here like the swine flu is loose, which is exactly what we want him to do.

This menu works great, because we've only got three items to worry about. We start with chicken pot stickers, which are my absolute favorite—I love the garlic and ginger. Since pot stickers are light, we need that flatbread to absorb the liquor (mother's helpers): there's nothing like pizza for the job. The special surprise is how the sweet figs and blue cheese combine with the peppery arugula. And for the grand finale—drumroll, please—the amazing "Flower Power." I had a version of this drink while on the road, and I just had to steal it and remix it. It was good, but it needed Gina flair! So *enjoy,* ladies, and here's to *girl power*!

PAT ON GIRLS' NIGHT

Okay, guys . . . this night is not for you unless you are going to "help out." "Girls' night out" in our home means "girls' night in." If you want things to run smoothly (both during and after the party), help your sweetie prepare some delicious treats . . . and then *get lost.* They don't want you around, and, trust me, you don't want to be around. As my father used to tell me, "If you get more than three women in a room, then you need to find another room to be in, or go take a very long drive." That was some of the best advice he ever gave me.

Chicken Pot Stickers

GINA These pot stickers are ideal appetizers for the ladies. They look like cute little presents. They can be prepared early and kept warm for serving. They're also flavored with soy, sesame, and a bit of our Neely "medicine"—cayenne pepper. Finally, they're made with ginger—a tonic of sorts to settle our stomachs after the cocktails and conversation. **SERVES 4 TO 6** *(about 30 to 36 pot stickers)*

½ pound ground chicken

¼ cup finely chopped green onions, plus more for garnish

1 clove garlic, finely chopped

2 teaspoons freshly grated peeled ginger

2 teaspoons soy sauce, plus more for dipping

2 teaspoons roasted sesame oil

⅛ teaspoon cayenne pepper

1 package (about 30 to 36) square wonton wrappers (found in the refrigerated section of grocery stores)

Canola oil, for sautéing

1 cup chicken broth

Combine the ground chicken, green onions, garlic, ginger, soy sauce, sesame oil, and cayenne pepper in a medium bowl, and mix well.

Lay one wonton wrapper at a time out on your work surface. (Cover the others with a damp paper towel to keep them from drying out.) Use your finger to brush the edges of the wrapper lightly with water (to make it sticky). Place a scant teaspoon of the filling in the center of the wonton. Bring two opposite points together and seal, then bring the next two points together and twist and pleat the top, making a little purse. Repeat until all the filling has been used.

Pour the canola oil into a large skillet set over medium heat, just enough to cover the bottom of the pan. Once it's hot and shimmering, slip half the wontons into the pan. (Make sure they are not touching or too crowded—if so, divide them into smaller batches.) Cook for 2 minutes (to sear the bottoms). Carefully pour ½ cup of the chicken broth into the skillet, and bring to a boil. Cover the skillet, reduce the heat to low, and allow the dumplings to finish cooking by steaming, another 2 to 3 minutes. Once they're done, carefully remove the dumplings to a plate. Wipe out the skillet, and repeat with the remaining dumplings and broth.

Serve sprinkled with the chopped green onions, and with soy sauce for dipping.

Fig and Arugula Flatbread

GINA You could easily order pizza for delivery, but why not have flatbread instead, and cut it into little squares? You can just buy the dough from your local grocer (or your local pizzeria, if you ask nicely) and add in all the other ingredients. Ripe figs will turn your traditional pizza into an amazing party favorite. We absolutely love this dish: it's hearty yet light, fruity, and flavorful. If you find the taste of blue cheese too strong, you can always substitute a mild goat cheese, which has a creamy tang that also goes well with the figs. We add the handfuls of fresh arugula to the flatbread while it's still hot, to add a pop of bright peppery flavor and color. **SERVES 4**

All-purpose flour, for work surface

1 pound pizza dough, at room temperature

¼ cup olive oil

Pinch of crushed red-pepper flakes

Kosher salt and freshly ground black pepper to taste

6 figs, sliced into thin wedges

2 large handfuls baby arugula

4 ounces blue cheese, crumbled

Preheat the oven to 450 degrees F. Spray a large, heavy sheet tray with nonstick spray.

Lightly flour your work surface. Stretch and roll your pizza dough into an oval shape about 12 inches long and 7 inches wide. Brush the dough with a bit of olive oil, and season with red-pepper flakes, salt, and pepper.

Toss the figs with 1 tablespoon of olive oil in a bowl, seasoning with salt and pepper. Top the dough with half the arugula and all of the figs, and sprinkle with the blue cheese. Drizzle with just a bit more olive oil. Bake for 25 to 30 minutes, until the dough is puffed and crisp and the cheese has melted. Remove the pan from the oven, and top with another handful of arugula. Slice across into pieces.

Flower Power

I had my first taste of St-Germain liqueur while sipping a "Flower Sour" at the Essex House hotel in Manhattan. The drink was something of a revelation: it smelled floral but tasted like a complex combination of peach, grapefruit, and lychee. I later discovered that St-Germain liqueur was made from wild Alpine elderflowers! From what I understand, it's a long and tedious process to make it, and I think that's perfect, because ladies are a "special process" all their own. Most of my girls are vodka girls, so I try to make something with vodka, but my recipe has a special twist to it.

A wild and complicated drink? That sounds just about right for us, ladies!

MAKES 2 COCKTAILS

2 ounces vodka

1 ounce St-Germain elderflower
    liqueur

1 ounce simple syrup (see page 114)

1 ounce lemon juice

Dry champagne, for topping off

Twists of lemon, for garnish

Pour the vodka, elderflower liqueur, simple syrup, and lemon juice into an ice-filled cocktail shaker, and give it a good shake. Pour into martini glasses, top with champagne, and serve each with a lemon twist.

Mini-Moon

Instead of having a big shebang of a wedding, we were quietly married on a cruise ship, and spent our five-day honeymoon aboard the vessel after the ceremony. Being together in that little cabin suite was all we needed to be happy. Maybe because we valued this simplicity, in the ensuing years we've celebrated Mini-Moons long before we knew they had a name. A Mini-Moon is a lightweight, low-maintenance honeymoon that can happen at any time.

Let's face it: given our schedules and budgets, it's not always possible to get away for a real vacation. But you can't let your love get away. A Mini-Moon is the perfect time to shake free of all the other stuff and enjoy a moment with your spouse or partner. Come home from work, prepare a great meal, have a glass of wine, and spend the evening romancing each other. Ladies: light candles, put out fresh flowers, and get dressed up. Fellas—put down your phones, e-mail, and "crackberry"s! Be present and in the moment. Be gentle and loving with each other. Reflect on how you felt when you were dating, and how your heart stopped at the very mention of each other's names.

You can plan an entire weekend to rekindle things, but it doesn't have to be that complicated at all. Try serving up some great dishes, getting a cuddle on the sofa, or spending an evening on your patio, and we bet you'll find yourself celebrating the holiday many times a year, just like us.

A tip: this whole menu can be essentially made ahead of time. Cook the bacon and make your shrimp skewers, parboil your lobster, poach your peaches, and make the salad dressing the night before, and all you have to do the night of is light up your grill and finish everything off.

(If you follow this formula with this menu, you will not be disappointed. Trust me, ladies, I speak from experience, and Big Daddy has never disappointed me.)

Grilled Bacon-Wrapped Shrimp with Sweet and Spicy Orange Dipping Sauce

Smoky bacon wrapped around shrimp spiced with Neely's barbecue rub and garlic creates a sensuous dance of flavors on your tongue. But the real romance of the dish is that you can feed your partner these bite-sized delights. **SERVES 4 AS A STARTER**

¼ cup olive oil

2 cloves garlic, roughly chopped

Juice of 1 lemon

1 teaspoon Neely's barbecue rub (see page 112)

Kosher salt and freshly ground black pepper

16 jumbo shrimp (about 1 pound), peeled and deveined

8 slices bacon, cut in half crosswise

8 bamboo skewers, soaked in water for 30 minutes

1 recipe sweet and spicy orange dipping sauce (recipe follows)

Preheat your grill to medium-high heat.

Whisk together the olive oil, garlic, lemon juice, Neely's barbecue rub, salt, and pepper together in a medium bowl. Add the shrimp, and toss. Cover with plastic wrap, and marinate for 15 minutes.

Cook your bacon in a large skillet over medium heat until halfway done (not yet crisp), about 3 to 4 minutes. Remove to a paper-towel-lined sheet tray to drain and cool.

Remove the shrimp from the marinade, and wrap the bacon slices around the center of each shrimp. Thread the skewer through the shrimp and bacon to secure. (Thread two shrimp per skewer.)

Grill the shrimp on both sides until the bacon is crisp and the shrimp are bright pink, about 5 to 7 minutes per side. Serve with the sweet and spicy orange dipping sauce.

SWEET AND SPICY ORANGE DIPPING SAUCE

MAKES ABOUT 1 CUP

¾ cup orange marmalade

¼ cup sweet Asian chile sauce

1 tablespoon soy sauce

Pinch of crushed red-pepper flakes

Mix all ingredients in a small bowl. Serve with the bacon-wrapped shrimp.

Green Herb Salad with Roasted Red Pepper Feta Dressing

Rich pink dressing and lovely greens give this salad a splash of color. Remember: what the eye sees translates to greater taste and greater overall pleasure.

SERVES 4 TO 6

ROASTED RED PEPPER FETA DRESSING

1/3 cup roughly chopped roasted red peppers

1/3 cup crumbled feta cheese

1/4 cup buttermilk

2 tablespoons sour cream

1 tablespoon red-wine vinegar

Kosher salt and freshly ground black pepper

HERB SALAD

4 ounces mixed baby greens

3 tablespoons torn fresh parsley leaves

3 tablespoons torn fresh dill

2 tablespoons torn fresh basil leaves

Combine all the dressing ingredients in a food processor, and pulse until smooth.

Toss the greens and herbs in a large salad bowl. Drizzle with the dressing, and toss. Serve immediately.

Grilled Lobsters with Lemon Basil Butter

GINA Can't have a Mini-Moon without my favorite seafood. Lobster, lobster, lobster . . . Some people find it too expensive, but isn't your relationship worth it? If you are going to splurge, then splurge on your biggest investment. Dip it in the drawn butter, feed it to your honey, and let your imagination run wild. **SERVES 2**

Kosher salt

Two 1½-pound live soft-shell lobsters (see note)

1 tablespoon olive oil

Freshly ground black pepper to taste

1 stick (½ cup) butter, melted

¼ teaspoon minced garlic

Zest of 1 lemon

1 tablespoon chopped fresh basil

Bring a large stockpot of water to a rolling boil. Add a generous handful of kosher salt, and add the lobsters. Boil for about 6 minutes, until the lobsters are beginning to turn red. Remove the lobsters from the water with tongs, and reserve until cool enough to handle. (We parcook our lobsters before grilling, so they can cook evenly and all the way through.)

Preheat a charcoal grill to medium heat.

Once the lobsters have cooled, use a pair of kitchen shears or a very sharp knife to split each lobster completely in half through the entire shell and flesh, starting from the tail end and working your way through the body. It will be easiest to use your chef's knife to split the thickest part of the lobster. Give the claws a whack with the back of your knife to break open a portion of the shell. This will allow the meat to be exposed to the smokiness and heat of the grill. Once they're halved, use a spoon to scoop out and discard the tomalley from each half (the green gunk—the stomach and intestinal tract).

Brush the exposed lobster meat with olive oil, and season with salt and pepper. Grill the lobster halves, exposed meat side down on the grill, for 4 minutes, until they're lightly charred and the meat is opaque and cooked through. Remove the lobster pieces to a platter.

Mix the hot melted butter with the garlic, lemon zest, basil, salt, and pepper. Drizzle the butter over the tails, and serve remaining butter on the side.

NOTE When buying live lobsters, look for lively guys who will curl their tails and wiggle when you pick them up. Splitting the lobsters before grilling may seem like a hassle, but it makes it easier to eat so you have more time to enjoy each other, rather than wrestle with your

food! We like to use charcoal in this recipe, because the lobster will only be on the grill for a short period of time and the charcoal adds just enough of that smoky flavor. Soft shells are easier to split in half, but if all you can find are hard-shell lobsters, use a sharp chef's knife to split their bodies—and be careful!

Poached Peaches and Cream

GINA Peaches are one of my favorite fruits, and cream always complements them. This dessert is refreshing and light: you don't want to get your man too full, or else you will be watching him sleep. The sweet champagne and fresh vanilla will relax his senses just enough. **SERVES 4**

4 firm ripe peaches

2 cups sweet champagne (labeled *demi sec*)

½ cup sugar

1 vanilla bean, split, seeded

Freshly whipped heavy cream, for topping

Bring a pot of water to a boil.

Make small "X"s on the bottom of the peaches with a sharp knife. Drop them into the pot of boiling water and leave them in for about 15 to 20 seconds, so their skins will loosen. Remove the peaches with a slotted spoon, and allow them to cool. Peel the peaches, slice them in half, and remove the pits.

Bring the champagne, sugar, and vanilla bean and seeds to a boil in a medium saucepan, stirring to dissolve the sugar. Reduce heat, and simmer for 5 minutes. Slip in the peach halves, and poach for 5 minutes, or until tender. Remove the vanilla bean, and transfer the peaches to a serving dish along with the champagne syrup. Let cool completely before serving. Top with freshly whipped cream.

NOTE You want to avoid overly ripe peaches for this recipe. They need to have a touch of firmness to them, or they will turn out mushy.

September

LABOR DAY

Seven-Layer Dip

Pat's Smoked Chicken

Green Pasta Salad

Smoky Corn and Zucchini Salad

Sparkling Raspberry Lemonade

BACK TO SCHOOL

Smokin' Snack Mix

All-Nighter Trail Mix

Rise and Shine Granola

Labor Day

We do a lot of eating in the South on both Memorial Day and Labor Day. They start and end the summer for us, and we're usually at the house with the grill or the smoker all fired up—and it's always so damn *hot*. Throughout the day, family and friends stop by for a meal.

But once you get to Labor Day, a busy day, you find Memphians don't want to battle the blazing-hot weather while standing over a 250-degree barbecue pit. (This was never a problem for Pat, because it wasn't an option: Neely's Bar-B-Que was definitely going to be open for business.) These days, because of the show, it's difficult for us to be in the restaurant. But people expect us to have barbecue on the menu anyway on Labor Day, so it's nice to shake them up a little bit with this smoked chicken. And pulling together some fresh salads and a refreshing beat-the-heat beverage is the ticket to get you out of the hot kitchen.

PAT'S LABOR OF LOVE

One year we'd just finished filming *Road Tasted with the Neelys,* and I told Gina that I was really missing our restaurant, Neely's Bar-B-Que. So, for Labor Day, I wanted to go back and be in there with the crew. For several weeks leading up to the holiday, I psyched myself up. These days, Gina and I really have to gear up before going into one of our restaurants, because so many people travel from all parts of the country to dine at one of them and maybe have a chance to visit with us.

I arrived at our downtown restaurant around 9 a.m., before opening hours, to get warmed up with the staff. When the doors opened, I was in a nice groove with the kitchen staff, churning out orders. Around noon, I got thirsty, so I headed to the wait station for some water. One of our customers spotted me there and asked for a photo. Well, the next thing you know, someone else wanted a picture, and soon cameras were flashing like I was in Times Square! The wait staff, who earlier had been happy to see me, now wanted to see me out of the dining room! I knew then that it was time for me to go, because my staff had work to do and I was getting in their way. Once I got outside, more people followed; I signed every autograph as graciously as I could and jumped into my truck. I called Tony from my cell phone and told him how lucky he, Mark, and Gaelin were to still be able to enjoy spending time in Neely's Bar-B-Que. I wish all of you a Labor of Love like that.

Seven-Layer Dip

Since Labor Day is a holiday when most are off work, people are always stopping by the Neely house, and we've got to have something at the ready for our guests to munch on. This seven-layer dip is absolutely beautiful as well as flavorful, a great item to set up to get the party started! **SERVES 4 TO 6 AS AN APPETIZER**

One 15-ounce can reduced-fat refried beans

1 chipotle pepper packed in adobo, minced

2 tablespoons water

1 cup shredded Monterey Jack cheese

One 4.5-ounce can chopped green chiles

1 avocado, pitted, peeled, and diced

2 plum tomatoes, seeded and chopped

1 cup sour cream

2 tablespoons roughly chopped fresh cilantro

Tortilla chips, for serving

Heat the refried beans, minced chipotle pepper, and water in a medium saucepan until hot and smooth. Spoon into a glass bowl or dish. Create a layer with all the cheese, then layers of all the chiles, avocado, tomatoes, sour cream, and cilantro, in that order. Serve with tortilla chips while the beans are warm, so that the cheese is nicely melted.

Pat's Smoked Chicken

PAT: Y'all know I've got to be smoking something for every summer holiday. No hickory chips for this bird: apple chips soaked in water and spread over hot charcoal will create a sweet, smoky flavor that's just right. This citrus marinade works well with the apple chips, and will keep the bird nice and moist. **SERVES 4**

One 3½-pound chicken

⅓ cup freshly squeezed lemon juice

⅓ cup freshly squeezed lime juice

⅓ cup freshly squeezed orange juice

¼ cup olive oil

3 cloves garlic, smashed and peeled

2 tablespoons chopped fresh rosemary leaves, plus 4 whole sprigs

2 tablespoons kosher salt

1 teaspoon freshly ground black pepper

Apple-wood chips, soaked for 1 hour

1 lemon, cut into wedges

Place the chicken in a large zip-top bag. Whisk together the next eight ingredients (except the sprigs of rosemary) in a measuring cup, and pour over the bird. Zip up the bag, and shake it to coat the chicken. Place the bag on a sheet tray, and leave in the fridge for 2 hours.

When you're ready to cook the chicken, preheat your grill to 225 degrees F, using a combination of charcoal and apple wood. When coals are ready, mound them to one side to create indirect heat.

Remove the chicken from the marinade and pat dry. Stuff the cavity with lemon wedges and rosemary sprigs.

Place the chicken on the grill over indirect heat, making sure it's well away from any flame. Cook, covered, for 2 hours. (Keep an eye on it to ensure that it maintains an even temperature.) Remove once the chicken has reached 160 degrees in the thickest part of the breast. The skin will be dark golden brown and the drumsticks will feel loose when you wiggle them. When the chicken is removed from the grill, tent it gently with foil. Let rest for 20 minutes before carving.

Green Pasta Salad

GINA Salad helps lighten the fare, and these green beans with cheese tortellini are a nice change from the traditional tossed salad. I am a big salad-eater, and there are a lot of women like me out there. Honey, we're trying to stay as "fabulous" as we can, eating all those greens. We just have to mix it up a bit so we don't get bored!

SERVES 4 TO 6

Kosher salt and freshly ground black pepper

2 cups ½-inch slices trimmed green beans

1 pound cheese tortellini, fresh or dried

⅓ cup pecans

2 cloves garlic, smashed and peeled

½ cup fresh basil leaves

½ cup fresh parsley leaves

½ cup fresh mint leaves

1 teaspoon crushed red-pepper flakes

½ cup shredded Parmesan cheese

Juice and zest of ½ lemon

½ cup extra-virgin olive oil

Prepare a large pot of salted boiling water, and a large bowl of ice water.

Blanch the green beans in the boiling water, 1 to 2 minutes. Remove the beans with a spider or tongs, and shock them in the large bowl of ice water to stop the cooking. Add the tortellini to the same pot of boiling water, and cook according to the package instructions. Drain well, and let cool.

Combine the pecans and garlic in the bowl of a food processor and pulse until chopped. Add basil, parsley, mint, red-pepper flakes, Parmesan, salt, pepper, and the lemon juice and zest, and pulse again until finely chopped. Drizzle in the olive oil while the motor is running, and blend until thoroughly combined.

Combine the green beans and tortellini in a serving bowl, and toss with the pesto. Serve at room temperature.

Smoky Corn and Zucchini Salad

Ready for a grilled salad? This late-summer mix will end your wait. No meat, just fresh, tasty grilled vegetables over baby arugula, basil, and cherry tomatoes.

SERVES 4 TO 6

2 medium zucchini, halved lengthwise

2 ears corn, husks removed

3 tablespoons extra-virgin olive oil, plus more for drizzling

Kosher salt and freshly ground black pepper

1 pint cherry tomatoes, halved lengthwise

1 pound fresh mozzarella mini-balls, halved

4 cups baby arugula

¼ cup fresh basil leaves, cut into a chiffonade

1 teaspoon Dijon mustard

2 tablespoons balsamic vinegar

¼ teaspoon crushed red-pepper flakes

Preheat the grill with charcoal to medium-high heat.

Drizzle the zucchini and corn with olive oil, and season with salt and pepper. Grill until tender and browned, rotating on occasion, for about 8 minutes. Let cool.

Slice the zucchini into half-moons about ¼ inch thick. Strip the kernels of corn off the cob. Put the corn and zucchini in a bowl, and toss with the cherry tomatoes, mozzarella balls, arugula, and basil.

Whisk together the mustard and balsamic vinegar, and trickle in the 3 tablespoons olive oil; mix in the crushed red-pepper flakes, and season with salt and pepper. Drizzle over the veggies, and toss. Season to taste and serve.

Sparkling Raspberry Lemonade

PAT One of the things I truly love about Gina is that she is *so* creative when it comes to beverages. This lemonade is as sparkling, stimulating, and sexy as my darling wife. The seltzer water gives this refresher a great bubbly taste. Gina uses raspberries, but you can substitute any fruit you love and you'll still be singing, "Oh, happy day!" **SERVES 8**

4 cups fresh raspberries

1½ cups sugar

1½ cups water

Two 1-inch strips lemon zest

2 cups freshly squeezed lemon juice

2 liters seltzer water, chilled

Put the raspberries, sugar, water, and lemon strips in a medium saucepan, and bring the liquid to a boil, stirring frequently so the sugar can dissolve and the fruit can soften. When it reaches the boil, turn off the heat and allow the mixture to steep for 10 minutes.

Strain the syrup through a fine sieve, and press on solids to extract all the juice and pulp from the berries. Discard the seeds and lemon strips. Refrigerate the syrup for 30 minutes, or until chilled.

Pour the chilled raspberry-lemon syrup and the lemon juice into a tall, large glass pitcher. Stir with a wooden spoon, then top with seltzer water. Serve in ice-filled glasses.

Back to School

GINA Boy, talk about mixed emotions: glad to see my kids growing up, but hating to let them go. As mothers, we want to protect our kids forever, but now's the time when you get to see if they were listening to you all these years. It's the test that all mothers talk about. So, when they're heading to college, or back to high school, you want to package up a little bit of home for them to take with them. We all remember how hard it was to keep eating right when we first left home. So send your little cubs off to school with just the right amount of tasty, healthy gut-filler to keep their tanks full and their minds and bodies energized. These mixes are easy to share, too, to help break the ice of new friendships. If you're making packed lunches, another trick is to slice up a Granny Smith apple, coat it with a dusting of cinnamon sugar, and pop it into a zip-top bag for a healthy sweet. (Or, if your kids are like Shelbi, the apple alone will do just fine!)

HALF-DOZEN AND A MOTHER

PAT When I was growing up, my mother had *six* kids to get ready for school every year. I could see the desperation in her eyes as the school year started: purchasing school supplies, lunch boxes, and school clothes and setting schedules were her biggest worries. I, on the other hand, was always excited, because I couldn't wait to kick off football season. But Mom would say, "If your grades drop, so will your football-playing time." And that was always enough motivation to keep me studying.

Mama Neely didn't play about bedtime hours, either. She used to say, "When you wake up, I want you bright-eyed and bushy-tailed!" Having to get a half-dozen kids ready every morning, and then getting yourself ready for work, must have been a *monster*! Thank God, Gina and I only had *two*, and they were girls, to add cream to this pie. Each year, these two sweethearts effortlessly make the transition from summertime to schooltime. Of course, they've had two parents to share the responsibilities. Gina and I have always worked as a team, and Spenser and Shelbi knew to get with the program!

Smokin' Snack Mix

This is a great mix of pretzel sticks, smoked almonds, and sesame sticks. Melting the butter and adding it to the mix helps the savory-sweet-spicy seasonings stick together. (And that little hint of cayenne will keep them awake!) Bag these up so that they can be taken to class for a power snack. **MAKES 7 CUPS**

3 cups thin pretzel sticks

One 10-ounce can roasted smoked almonds

2 cups sesame sticks

4 tablespoons (½ stick) butter, melted

3 tablespoons light-brown sugar

1 tablespoon Neely's barbecue rub (see page 112)

½ teaspoon cayenne pepper

Preheat the oven to 250 degrees F.

Toss the pretzels, almonds, and sesame sticks in a large bowl. Melt the butter in a saucepan, and whisk in the brown sugar, barbecue rub, and cayenne pepper. Drizzle the butter mixture over the snack mix, and toss to coat.

Spread the snack mixture evenly over two rimmed sheet trays, and bake for 30 minutes, tossing and stirring the mixture halfway through cooking.

All-Nighter Trail Mix

This all-nighter mix is for those extended study groups or projects that go on and on, till eventually everyone is too lazy to go get something to eat. Our sweet, salty, and fruity combination will satisfy all their cravings, as well as keep them away from less healthy options (including coffee!). **MAKES ABOUT 6 CUPS**

1 cup roasted salted cashews

1 cup roasted pecans

1 cup dried cranberries

1 cup chopped dried apricots

1 cup candy-coated chocolates (M&M's are ideal)

1 cup dried banana chips

Toss all the ingredients in a large bowl. Divide between several zip-top plastic baggies.

Rise and Shine Granola

Filled with the energy of oats and the antioxidants of blueberries, this is the mix for a kick-ass day. Keep it on hand and nothing can stop you. What's nice is, it's not too sweet, not too fatty, and really flavorful. It's just right; and when you're away from your family or what's familiar to you, this kind of homemade love will soften the blow. **MAKES ABOUT 7 CUPS**

4 cups rolled oats

1½ cups chopped pecans

1 cup sweetened shredded coconut

½ cup vegetable oil

½ cup real maple syrup

2 tablespoons light-brown sugar

½ teaspoon kosher salt

1 cup dried blueberries

Preheat the oven to 350 degrees F.

Mix together the oats, pecans, and coconut in a large bowl. Whisk together the oil, syrup, brown sugar, and salt in a separate bowl. Pour the oil mixture over the rolled oats, and toss thoroughly.

Evenly spread out the oat mixture on two rimmed sheet trays. Bake for 20 minutes, stirring halfway through, until golden. Stir in the dried blueberries at the end of baking. Let cool completely before storing. The mix can be kept in an airtight container for up to a week.

October

NEIGHBORLY HOUSEWARMING

Just-Right Dry Rub for Steaks

Ancho-Spiced Nuts

Blue Ribbon Blueberry Muffins

HARVEST PARTY

Grilled Smoked Sausage and Pepper Sandwich

German Potato Salad

Pumpkin and Sweet Potato Bisque

Neighborly Housewarming

GINA Housewarming is an old, time-honored tradition that's in desperate need of a revival! We've gotten too far away from neighborly relationships (which is why I say the "village" in our society has been forgotten). When we were growing up, everybody knew everybody, and when people moved in, you welcomed them by bringing over food and introducing yourself and your family. Most people with kids like to move in the summertime, so they can get their house ready before the kids go back to school in September; so, rather than bombarding them just as they arrive, we like to extend our warm welcome sometime in early October, when they're starting to settle in for real.

So bring these gifts over, strike up a conversation, and, before you know it, your neighbor will be knocking on your door for a cup of sugar, or just to vent. . . . Remember those good ole days?

HOUSEWARMING FROM THE INSIDE

PAT When we purchased our first home—oh boy, it was something. We finally had a place of our own: the girls had their own rooms, there was a separate dining room, a nice backyard, and of course a decent kitchen, where Gina and I could do our "thang." It was a great feeling. Now, Gina is not a fan of moving, and to top it off, she was pregnant with Shelbi when we purchased our first home, in the dead heat of summer. So she got a pass on the packing-and-moving responsibilities. On moving day, I asked the movers to bring the sofa in first so that my sweetheart could immediately get off her feet while the movers and I unloaded the rest.

The second time we moved, there was no pregnancy . . . but still no Gina. Conveniently, the lady of the new house had scheduled a doctor's appointment for that day. Could it have had something to do with the move? I didn't really mind either time, because men are supposed to "handle the business," and y'all know all Gina has to say is "You did it, Big Daddy," and I become a cream puff.

It takes a few weeks to get settled in and empty most of the boxes, but once you do, it's time to get the party started. We start by inviting family and friends over to give them a tour, then we turn up the music and bring on the fellowship and great food, and everyone has a damn good time.

Just-Right Dry Rub for Steaks

Assure your neighbors that they won't have to dig out the grill immediately to slap this dry rub on steaks (although you wouldn't mind if they did!). The mixture can be kept in a clean, airtight jar for up to 3 months. **MAKES 1 CUP**

6 tablespoons kosher salt

2 tablespoons paprika

2 tablespoons freshly ground black pepper

2 tablespoons garlic powder

2 tablespoons onion powder

1 tablespoon ground thyme

1½ teaspoons cayenne pepper

Combine all the seasonings in a medium bowl, and whisk well. Use right away to season a steak, or scoop into a half-pint Mason jar for storage, or spoon into four 2-ounce spice jars, to give as gifts.

Ancho-Spiced Nuts

Everybody likes something to munch on for extra energy, or to accompany that glass of wine earned by a day of unpacking! You may think you'll never find ancho-chile powder, but McCormick packages it, and it is readily available at most grocery stores. It's really important to keep the heat on low in this recipe, because the nuts and spices are inclined to get too brown. **MAKES 2 CUPS**

4 tablespoons unsalted butter

1 cup pecans

1 cup cashews

2 teaspoons light-brown sugar

2 teaspoons ancho-chile powder

1 teaspoon kosher salt

½ teaspoon smoked paprika

½ teaspoon ground cumin

½ teaspoon freshly ground black pepper

Melt the butter in a large skillet over low heat. Stir in the nuts, the sugar, and the spices, and toast them together for about 6 minutes. Transfer to a sheet tray, and cool completely. Put the spiced nuts in a Mason jar, and tie with a bow to give as a gift.

Blue Ribbon Blueberry Muffins

Easy to transport and to eat while unpacking, these moist and dense muffins are more like little pound cakes with blueberries than your typical crumbly muffin. If blueberries are out of season and you want to use frozen ones (a perfectly fine option!), increase the oven temperature to 375 degrees F. **MAKES 12 MUFFINS**

2¼ cups all-purpose flour

1 tablespoon baking powder

½ teaspoon table salt

1 cup buttermilk, well shaken

1 teaspoon pure vanilla extract

1 stick (½ cup) unsalted butter, at room temperature

1 cup sugar, plus 2 tablespoons for the muffin tops

1 egg, at room temperature

1½ cups fresh blueberries

Preheat your oven to 350 degrees F. Put paper liners in a twelve-cup muffin tin.

Whisk together the flour, baking powder, and salt in a bowl. Measure out the buttermilk and stir the vanilla into it.

Beat the butter and the cup of sugar in the bowl of a standing mixer with the paddle attachment until light and fluffy, 3 to 4 minutes. Add the egg, and beat until combined. Scrape down the sides of the bowl.

Beat half the flour into the mixer bowl, then the buttermilk, then the remaining flour. Fold the blueberries in with a rubber spatula.

Divide the batter among the twelve muffin cups, and sprinkle the tops with the remaining 2 tablespoons of sugar. Bake for 25 minutes, or until a toothpick inserted into the center of a muffin comes out clean.

Harvest Party

PAT The fall in Memphis is beautiful, and we love it: the oppressive summer heat begins to fade, and, with the foliage just coming in, it's perfect weather for a party.

When the girls were younger, we would host an annual Halloween party at the restaurant. They would dress up in costumes and invite all of their friends and cousins for ghost stories, great food, and some real tricks and treats. Of course, those days are long gone, and we've had to find a way of keeping our traditional celebration alive—at least until we have some grandbabies. So now we throw a grown folks' Harvest Party instead of a strictly Halloween shindig. Y'all know, Gina is as festive as anyone that's ever lived, and she goes all-out, decorating the house in traditional orange and brown colors and putting a "Boo" mat at the front door. She purchases several pumpkins for the yard and a few smaller ones for inside, and I have to put my knife skills to work in a different way by carving them into creepy jokers and finding small candles to light them up. Gina always carves hers with a smile, which the kids call her out on every year. "What can I say?" she says innocently. "I'm all about the happiness on any occasion."

Our Harvest Party kicks off the holiday season and gets our family and friends ready for a fun-filled winter, so we put a menu together that celebrates fall vegetables to the fullest. (And in case you missed it, it also goes with Gina's seasonal orange-and-brown decor!)

Grilled Smoked Sausage and Pepper Sandwich

PAT I can eat grilled sausage all by itself: there is something about the mix of pork and spices that just makes my belly happy. Now, I can also eat grilled peppers and onions all by themselves—or as a veggie side dish. Combine the two, however, and it's "*Look out!*" (I like to add spicy Creole mustard for a little extra kick.) **SERVES 6**

1 red bell pepper, seeded, sliced into rings

1 yellow bell pepper, seeded, sliced into rings

1 orange bell pepper, seeded, sliced into rings

1 large red onion, sliced into rings

¼ cup olive oil

Kosher salt and freshly ground black pepper

½ cup Neely's BBQ sauce (see page 37), for brushing

2 pounds smoked sausages (such as kielbasa or smoked brats), sliced in half lengthwise, then in crosswise quarters

3 tablespoons chopped fresh parsley

Six 6-inch hero rolls, split lengthwise, toasted

Creole mustard, for serving

Prepare the grill to medium heat.

Toss the bell-pepper and onion slices with the olive oil, and season with salt and pepper. Grill the vegetables until tender and lightly charred, turning occasionally, for about 10 to 12 minutes. Brush with barbecue sauce for the last few minutes of grilling. Grill the sausages for 7 to 10 minutes, turning frequently, also brushing with barbecue sauce during the last few minutes of grilling.

Remove the veggies to a bowl, and toss with the chopped parsley. Grill the rolls until toasted. To assemble, divide grilled sausages and veggies among the rolls, and top with some Creole mustard.

German Potato Salad

A great dressing is the key to an outstanding potato salad. And let me tell you: in our version, this German lady is wearing a nice dress. Y'all know Gina dresses well, too, and once she adds her signature "pig," this salad is a stand-out, even among the best potato salads in Memphis. **SERVES 6**

⅓ cup white-wine vinegar

2 tablespoons sugar

2 tablespoons stone-ground mustard, or to taste

Kosher salt and freshly ground black pepper

2½ pounds Yukon Gold potatoes, well scrubbed, diced into 1-inch cubes

8 slices bacon, diced

1 medium red onion, chopped

2 cloves garlic, chopped

2 tablespoons chopped fresh dill

2 tablespoons chopped fresh parsley

Whisk together the white-wine vinegar, sugar, mustard, salt, and pepper to make the dressing.

Slip the potatoes into a large pot of cold water. Bring to a boil, add a large pinch of salt, then reduce to a simmer. Cook the potatoes for 20 minutes, or until fork-tender. Drain well, and keep warm while you prepare the bacon.

Cook the bacon in a large skillet over medium heat until crisp. Remove the bacon to a paper-towel-lined plate. Add the onion and garlic to the bacon grease, and sauté until tender, about 4 minutes. Whisk the dressing into the vegetables. Simmer, while stirring, until you see the dressing beginning to thicken so that it lightly coats the back of a spoon, about 2 minutes.

Add the potatoes, dill, parsley, and bacon to the pan, and stir together well to coat with dressing. Serve while warm.

Pumpkin and Sweet Potato Bisque

Fall is a perfect time to try this bisque. The healthy and delicious sweet potato, which certainly represents the season in our home, is one of the stars of the soup. And if you've got leftover pumpkin flesh after carving your decorations, you can always substitute that for the canned purée. Using chicken broth instead of water gives this thick soup a rich-tasting down-home flair. **SERVES 6**

4 slices bacon

1 medium Vidalia onion, chopped

2 cloves garlic, chopped

2 tablespoons finely grated peeled fresh ginger

½ teaspoon ground cinnamon

½ teaspoon ground allspice

Kosher salt and freshly ground black pepper to taste

6 cups chicken broth

One 15-ounce can pumpkin purée

3 large sweet potatoes, peeled and diced

1 cup heavy cream

½ teaspoon cayenne pepper

Chopped fresh chives, for garnish

Cook the bacon in a large, heavy pot over medium heat until the bacon is crisp and the fat is rendered, about 5 minutes. Remove the bacon with a slotted spoon to a paper-towel-lined plate, and reserve the bacon fat. Crumble the bacon when cool.

Sauté the onion, garlic, ginger, cinnamon, and allspice in the bacon fat until tender, about 5 minutes. Season the veggies with a bit of salt and pepper. Stir in the chicken broth and canned pumpkin, then add the sweet potatoes. Reduce the heat, and simmer for 15 minutes, or until the sweet potatoes are tender.

Use an immersion blender to purée the soup until smooth. Stir in the heavy cream, and season with the cayenne pepper. Serve with a garnish of bacon crumbles and chopped chives.

Game-Day Grilled Turkey Drumsticks

PAT Most people will serve chicken for tailgates, but you know we like to shake it up a bit, so we serve turkey legs—or "Fred Flintstone bones," as I like to call them. To give ours a kick, we let them marinate overnight in buttermilk, hot sauce, lemon, onion, and garlic. Then we take them out the next day, let the excess drip off, brush on the olive oil, and throw them on the grill. Folks will be asking for these so fast, you may never get to your business with the glaze. **SERVES 8**

2 cups buttermilk

2 tablespoons hot sauce, preferably Tabasco

Juice of 1 lemon

1 onion, sliced

4 cloves garlic, smashed and peeled

8 turkey drumsticks (14 to 16 ounces each; ask your butcher for them)

Olive oil, for drumsticks and grill

Kosher salt and freshly ground black pepper

1 recipe game-day glaze (recipe follows)

The night before the game, prepare the marinade: Whisk together the buttermilk, hot sauce, and lemon juice, and stir in the onion and garlic. Put the turkey legs in a large casserole dish, and pour the marinade over them. (You can also divide the drumsticks and the marinade between two large zip-top bags.) Cover with plastic wrap, and place in the refrigerator overnight.

On game day, preheat your grill to medium heat.

Remove the turkey legs from the marinade, and allow the extra to drip off. Brush the turkey legs with olive oil, and season with salt and pepper. Rub the grill grates with oil, using a clean tea towel or a crumpled-up paper towel. Grill the turkey drumsticks, turning to cook on all sides, for about 15 minutes, until the skin is crisp and golden. Cover the grill, and continue cooking for another 25 minutes, rotating occasionally to prevent the legs from burning. Brush with the game-day glaze, and cook, turning often, for 10 more minutes.

GAME-DAY GLAZE

The great thing about this glaze is that it can be used for any grilled meat. You can brush it onto pork chops, chicken, ribs—anything you feel like grilling on game day! **MAKES ABOUT ½ CUP**

2 tablespoons butter

½ small onion, minced

¼ cup apple-cider vinegar

¼ cup molasses

2 tablespoons ketchup

1 tablespoon yellow mustard

½ teaspoon cayenne pepper

Dash of Worcestershire sauce

Dash of hot sauce, preferably Tabasco

Kosher salt and freshly ground black pepper

Melt the butter in a medium sauté pan over medium heat. Add the onion, and sauté until soft, about 3 minutes. Stir in the vinegar, molasses, ketchup, mustard, cayenne, Worcestershire, and hot sauce. Season with salt and pepper. Simmer over medium heat for 10 minutes, so all the flavors can marry.

Beer-Braised Brisket Chili

GINA I can hear "It's a Man's World" by James Brown playing whenever I make this chili. But beer, bacon, and brisket are three of my favorite "b"s, too. So don't be scared, ladies—this delicious chili will please the whole family, not just your quarterbacks. As with most stews and chilis, this is best made the night before, and reheated right before the big game starts! **SERVES 8 TO 10**

5 slices bacon, chopped

One 5-pound brisket of beef, trimmed, cut into 1-inch cubes

1 tablespoon kosher salt

2 teaspoons freshly ground black pepper

1 large red onion, finely chopped

4 cloves garlic, finely chopped

1 small jalapeño pepper, seeds removed, finely chopped

2 tablespoons chile powder

2 tablespoons tomato paste

12 ounces beer, preferably Budweiser

One 32-ounce can diced tomatoes, with juices

2 chipotle peppers packed in adobo sauce, chopped

2 tablespoons adobo sauce

Two 15-ounce cans pinto beans, drained and rinsed

Pepper-Jack cheese, shredded, for serving

Tortilla chips, crushed, for serving

Avocados, diced, for serving

Fresh cilantro, chopped, for serving

Cook the bacon in a large Dutch oven over medium-high heat until the bacon is crisp and the fat is rendered, about 6 minutes. While the bacon is cooking, season the cubed brisket with salt and pepper. Remove bacon to a paper-towel-lined plate. Brown the brisket, in batches, on all sides, until it has a nice color and a crust forms on the outside of the meat (about 8 to 10 minutes per batch). Remove the brisket to a rimmed plate.

Sauté the onion, garlic, and jalapeño in the pot until tender and fragrant, about 4 minutes. Stir in the chile powder, and toast for just a minute with the onions and garlic. Mix in the tomato paste, then pour in the beer. Bring to a boil, scraping up all the tasty brown bits on the bottom of the pot with a wooden spoon. Add the tomatoes and their juices, the chipotle and adobo sauce, and, finally, the browned brisket and any accumulated juices. Bring the pot to a boil, reduce the heat to medium-low, and simmer, partially covered, for $2\frac{1}{2}$ hours, or until the brisket is nice and tender.

Remove the cover, and add the beans and reserved bacon. Cook for 30 more minutes. Taste for seasoning, and adjust with salt and pepper. Serve in bowls topped with cheese, crushed tortilla chips, diced avocado, and cilantro.

Roasted Corn on a Stick

Corn on a stick? Did somebody say big-kid treat? Don't forget the mayo: you'll need to make the chile powder and cayenne stick. No grill? No worries, you can go the old-school route with a hot cast-iron skillet. **SERVES 8**

8 ears corn, husks removed

Olive oil, for rubbing corn

Seasoned salt to taste

8 heavy wooden skewers

½ cup mayonnaise

1 teaspoon chile powder

¼ teaspoon cayenne pepper

Kosher salt and freshly ground black pepper

Heat a large cast-iron skillet or griddle over medium-high heat. Rub the corn generously with olive oil, and season with seasoned salt to taste. Cook the corn, in batches, until it's cooked through and lightly charred on all sides, rotating, for about 6 to 8 minutes. When it's cool enough to handle, push a wooden skewer into the cob of each ear of corn to make a handle.

Meanwhile, mix the mayonnaise, chile powder, cayenne, and salt and pepper to taste in a small bowl. Brush the hot corn with the mayonnaise mixture.

Pat's Quarterback Cookies

GINA My man is the quarterback of the house—and I love him for it! He may call the plays, but when he does, I execute the sweetness all over the field. The dark-brown sugar gives these cookies the toasty football color, and the coconut, toffee-candy bits, and pecans will keep him from getting sacked.

Who wrote *that* play, Coach? Maybe you should put me in!

MAKES ABOUT 4 DOZEN COOKIES

2 cups all-purpose flour

½ teaspoon baking soda

¾ teaspoon table salt

1 cup unsalted butter, at room temperature

1 cup granulated white sugar

¾ cup packed dark-brown sugar

2 eggs

1 teaspoon pure vanilla extract

1 cup semisweet chocolate chips

1 cup sweetened flaked coconut

¾ cup toffee-candy bits

½ cup chopped pecans, toasted

Preheat the oven to 350 degrees F, and adjust the racks to the middle. Line two heavy baking sheets with parchment paper.

Whisk together the flour, baking soda, and salt in a medium bowl. In a standing mixer, cream together the butter and the sugars until light and fluffy. Beat in the eggs, one at a time, and add the vanilla. Scrape down the sides of the mixing bowl with a rubber spatula, making sure everything is evenly mixed together. Add the dry ingredients, and mix until well blended. Turn off the mixer, and stir in the chocolate chips, coconut, toffee, and pecans by hand.

Drop the cookie dough, in tablespoon batches, onto prepared sheets, leaving about 2 inches of space between the cookies. Bake cookies until golden brown, about 13 to 15 minutes. Remove, and let cool completely on the cookie sheets.

Giving Thanks

PAT This is big, y'all! Big food, big guest list, big fun, big table, big plates, and, at the end, big bellies. There's no other holiday that says *food* like Thanksgiving. I have no idea how our home became Thanksgiving headquarters for the Neely clan, but it has, and we love it. We have hosted as many as fifty or more people on Turkey Day. Is that insane or what? In some ways, having all those folks around reminds me of the holidays we used to spend at one of our grandparents' homes—houses that appeared to be as small as shoe boxes but were as comfortable as king-sized beds. It was all about the delicious food and the warm, loving spirit that filled the house.

In that vein, Gina launched a tradition several years ago that has become something of a highlight for all of us. Before we sit down for dinner, all the people present (especially the kids) gather in a circle and must say something they are truly thankful for. It helps us keep in perspective how truly *blessed* we are. Once dinner is over, everyone pitches in to clean the kitchen; then the guys retire to a room for a good football game and some belly rubbing. Gina and the women usually retire to the living room for music and booty shaking. I guess it's their way of working off the turkey and dressing.

If you have a family as large as ours, you might want to double the recipe quantities. Because you know they'll be back for seconds.

GINA'S THANKFUL PATH

Thanksgiving meant a lot to our family when I was growing up. It was also a holiday that had a big impact on my spiritual growth. I loved seeing everyone smiling, laughing, cracking jokes, dancing, and just being plain ole delightful. At Thanksgiving, it seemed everything was cooked more carefully, as though you were not only supposed to see the love but taste it as well.

When I grew up and was blessed with my own family, I made creating the same type of environment a priority. I want to be able to rewind the tape and join with everyone on Cella Street again. We follow the same traditions now that we did then, and I hope my daughters are watching. Isn't that what life is all about? Keeping traditions alive from generation to generation, so that the path to being truly thankful will stay clear for your loved ones.

Memphis Fried Turkey

GINA Fried turkey was and is very big in the South. I watched Mama Callie make it many a time, and I was always thinking she was going to burn herself or the house down! She'd rub the spice mixture all over the turkey and into the cavity. (Hmm . . . I always thought Pat was the first spice-rub master, but maybe not.) When you fry a turkey, you are sealing all those herb flavors and juices right in. You also get outrageously crispy skin. Pat likes to fry with peanut oil, because of its high smoke temperature and great flavor. Try it; it's easier than you think (see note on page 245), and leaves your oven free for all your side dishes! **SERVES 10**

1 tablespoon smoked paprika

1 tablespoon kosher salt

1½ teaspoons garlic powder

1½ teaspoons freshly ground black pepper

1½ teaspoons onion powder

1 teaspoon cayenne pepper

1 teaspoon dried thyme

One 14-pound turkey, giblets removed, washed and dried

3 or more gallons peanut oil, for frying (see note)

Mix the smoked paprika, salt, garlic powder, black pepper, onion powder, cayenne pepper, and thyme together in a bowl. Sprinkle some of the spice rub inside the cavity of the turkey. Separate the skin from the breast meat by using one or two fingers, starting at the top of the breast and gently sliding to the right and left, then working down. (So as not to tear the skin, nails trimmed and rings off! Or you can use a surgical glove.) Massage the rub onto the meat underneath the skin with your hands. Sprinkle the remaining rub on the turkey's skin. Place the turkey on a large sheet tray, and cover with plastic wrap. Refrigerate overnight, or up to 24 hours, so the flavors can marry.

Fill your turkey fryer with peanut oil, and preheat to 400 degrees F (it will take about 1 hour for the oil to come to temperature). (For tips on deep-frying, see note on facing page.)

Remove the turkey from the refrigerator, and let it come to room temperature as your oil heats.

Once the oil is hot, very carefully lower the turkey into the hot oil. (Most turkey fryers come with a basket for the turkey that has hooks and a handle to lower and lift. If yours doesn't, get yourself a long set of sturdy tongs to grip deep the inside cavity and breast, as well as an industrial kitchen fork to hold the back side of the bird.) Make sure the oil maintains its temperature while frying. Fry the turkey until the skin is dark golden brown and crisp, or until the internal temperature of the breast reaches 155 degrees F on an instant-read thermometer, about 45 minutes. Carefully remove the turkey from the oil, and let it rest and drain on a wire rack about 30 minutes. Do not cover the turkey with foil or it will lose some of its crispness. The internal temperature will rise to 165 degrees while resting.

Transfer the turkey to a serving platter, and serve.

NOTE Before you begin, check out our deep-frying guide on page 19 for general frying tips. The size of your turkey will determine how much oil you need to fill your fryer. The safest way to figure that out is to place the raw turkey in the empty fryer and then cover with clean cold water. Remove the turkey; note where the water comes to in the pot (no more than three-quarters full, or get a bigger pot!), and mark with a pen. Empty the fryer of water, and dry it very well.

Fill the fryer up with oil to the line you marked, being careful not to fill it more than three-quarters of the way. This will ensure that the hot oil does not spill out over the top of the fryer and cause a fire! (Always keep an extra empty pot and a large ladle next to you while you fry the turkey, just in case. If it looks like it might bubble over, just scoop some of the oil out.)

Most people use propane and a deep pot set up in their backyard, but you can now purchase countertop electric fryers large enough to do the job more safely indoors (and out of the cold air). These fryers come with pre-marked levels for the oil and can be covered with a lid.

ALTERNATIVE

Oven-Roasted Turkey

To roast the turkey, set the rack at the lowest position in the oven and heat to 325 degrees F. Remove the turkey from the refrigerator to bring to room temperature. Tie the legs together, and tuck the wing tips under.

Place the turkey in a large roasting pan. Drizzle the outside of the turkey with a few tablespoons of olive oil, and sprinkle with salt and pepper. Roast the turkey for about 3 hours, or until a thermometer inserted into the thickest part of the thigh registers 165 degrees F. Transfer the turkey to a platter, cover loosely with foil, and let rest for 30 minutes before carving.

Corn Bread and Collard Dressing

GINA This dish is the "queen of dressing," because dressing and collards are two favorites of mine. I add bacon, 'cause you gotta have some pig, and the carrots give it a different spin from your traditional dish.

You'll want to think ahead with this recipe and make that corn bread the day before. It needs to be dry enough to soak up all the good flavors. **SERVES 10 TO 12**

6 slices bacon, chopped

1 small bunch collard greens, ribs removed, sliced into very thin ribbons

1 large onion, finely chopped

1 large carrot, finely chopped

2 stalks celery, finely chopped

3 cloves garlic, chopped

1 tablespoon chopped fresh thyme

1/4 teaspoon crushed red-pepper flakes

Kosher salt and freshly ground black pepper

8 cups cubed day-old yellow cornbread (see page 23)

4 cups chicken broth

2 eggs, beaten

1/4 cup chopped fresh parsley

Preheat the oven to 375 degrees F, and butter a 4-quart casserole.

Cook the bacon in a large, heavy skillet set over medium heat until the bacon is crisp and the fat has rendered. Remove the bacon with a slotted spoon, and discard all but 2 tablespoons of the bacon fat. Sauté the vegetables, garlic, and thyme in the hot bacon fat until tender, about 8 minutes. Season with the red-pepper flakes, salt, and pepper, and set aside to cool slightly.

While the vegetables are cooking, spread the corn-bread cubes on a baking sheet and toast in the hot oven for 5 to 6 minutes, until they brown slightly on the edges.

Put the cubed corn bread in a very large mixing bowl. Pour the broth and beaten eggs over the corn bread. Add the vegetable mixture, bacon, and parsley, and toss all together. Spoon the dressing into the prepared casserole dish, and cover with foil. Bake for 30 minutes; then uncover and continue baking for 15 minutes more, to give it a nice crust.

The Best Mashed Potatoes

The key word here is "Gouda": it takes your mashed potatoes right to the VIP list. This way, please! **SERVES 6 TO 8**

2½ pounds Yukon Gold potatoes, well scrubbed, cut into quarters

Kosher salt and freshly ground black pepper

½ cup (1 stick) butter

¾ cup half-and-half

1 cup shredded smoked Gouda

¼ cup thinly sliced fresh chives

Slip the potatoes into a large pot of cold salted water, and bring to a boil. Reduce heat, and simmer for 15 to 20 minutes, until tender.

Meanwhile, heat butter and half-and-half in a small pot until the butter melts and the mixture is hot.

Once the potatoes are cooked, drain well in a colander and then return to the large pot. Turn the heat back on to low, and stir the potatoes to extract moisture from them. Mash the potatoes until smooth, and stir in the hot cream and butter. Add the shredded cheese by the handful, stirring to melt, and season generously with salt and pepper. Stir in the sliced chives. Serve immediately.

Sautéed Kale with Garlic

GINA Kale is my newest and most charming friend. It's in the green-veggie family, but is often overlooked. Boy, are you guys missing out on this one. Preparing it is very easy: all you do is chop some garlic, sauté it in some olive oil with red-pepper flakes for a kick, add in some salt, pepper, and broth, and steam. Now, we all can use an easy dish to prepare on such a busy day . . . so I gift you with this one. **SERVES 6 TO 8**

¼ cup olive oil

5 cloves garlic, thinly sliced

½ teaspoon crushed red-pepper flakes

2 pounds kale (about 3 large bunches), well washed, stems discarded, roughly chopped

Kosher salt and freshly ground black pepper

¼ cup chicken broth

Juice of ½ lemon

Heat the olive oil in a large Dutch oven over medium heat. Add the garlic and red-pepper flakes, and cook until the edges of the garlic turn golden brown, about 2 minutes. Add the kale in handfuls, and stir and toss with a pair of tongs, adding more as they wilt down. Season with salt and pepper, and continue to sauté for about 5 minutes. Add the chicken broth to the pot, cover with lid, and steam for 10 to 12 minutes, until the kale is very soft and tender. Remove the lid, add the lemon juice, and serve.

Cranberry Chipotle Relish

GINA This is not your off-the-shelf variety of cranberry sauce, although that can work in a pinch (remember my emergency run to the store during my first Thanksgiving at Mama Neely's?). In this recipe I'm talking sweet, zesty, spicy, and savory: you don't know whether to slow-dance or cut a jig. I say mix it all up, just like the relish, and let it go. **MAKES 3½ CUPS**

2 tablespoons butter

1 small shallot, finely chopped

Kosher salt

1 cup golden raisins

12 ounces fresh cranberries, rinsed

½ cup fresh orange juice

½ cup water

1 cup sugar

1 chipotle pepper packed in adobo
    sauce, minced

Melt the butter in a medium saucepan over medium heat until it foams. Toss in the shallot, and sauté until soft, about 2 minutes. Season the shallot with a touch of salt. Stir in the raisins, cranberries, orange juice, water, sugar, and chipotle pepper, and bring to a boil. Reduce heat, and simmer, stirring on occasion, for 15 minutes. Let cool to room temperature, and refrigerate for at least 30 minutes until ready to serve.

Apple Crumb Pie

Now, here's an old faithful; every Thanksgiving spread requires a great apple pie. Not a whole lot to say about it—it's tasty, of course—but the crumb topping takes this pie up a notch. It's as though you added a leopard-skin belt to your little black dress. The brown sugar, cinnamon, and allspice don't hurt, either.   **SERVES 8**

PIE DOUGH

- 1½ cups plus 2 tablespoons all-purpose flour, plus more for rolling
- 2 tablespoons granulated white sugar
- ½ teaspoon table salt
- 8 tablespoons (1 stick) cold unsalted butter, cut into small pieces
- 2 tablespoons vegetable shortening
- 3 to 4 tablespoons ice water, or as needed

For the pie dough: Pulse the flour with the sugar and salt in a food processor. Add the butter and shortening, and pulse just until the mixture resembles coarse meal. Add the ice water, and process until the dough just starts to form a ball. Transfer the dough to a floured work surface, and knead gently for 1 minute. Pat the dough into a disk, wrap in plastic, and refrigerate for at least 1 hour. (The crust can be prepared a day ahead. Soften slightly at room temperature before rolling out.)

On a lightly floured work surface, roll out the dough to an 11-inch round, about ¼ inch thick. Transfer dough to a 9-inch ceramic or glass deep-dish pie pan, and roll a rolling pin over the pan to trim the overhang. Using a fork, prick the bottom of the pie shell all over, and refrigerate until firm, at least 20 minutes.

Preheat the oven to 350 degrees F.

FILLING

4 medium Granny Smith apples, peeled, cored, and sliced into ½-inch wedges

4 medium Golden Delicious apples, peeled, cored, and sliced into ½-inch wedges

Juice of 1 lemon

¾ cup granulated white sugar

2 tablespoons all-purpose flour

½ teaspoon ground cinnamon

½ teaspoon ground allspice

⅛ teaspoon freshly grated nutmeg

Pinch of table salt

CRUMB TOPPING

1 cup all-purpose flour

½ cup rolled oats

½ packed cup light-brown sugar

¼ teaspoon ground cinnamon

¼ teaspoon ground allspice

Pinch of table salt

½ cup (1 stick) butter, cut into small cubes

½ cup chopped pecans

For the filling: Toss the apples, lemon juice, sugar, flour, cinnamon, allspice, nutmeg, and salt in a large bowl. Let the apple mixture sit out at room temperature for 10 minutes, then mound it in the pie shell.

For the topping: Mix the flour, oats, brown sugar, cinnamon, allspice, and salt in a large bowl. Cut the butter into the mixture until it forms pea-sized lumps. Stir in the pecans.

To assemble: Sprinkle the crumb topping on top of the mounded filling in the chilled pie crust, and place on a sheet tray. (The dish will be so full that you may need to press the topping on around the edges. Juice will definitely overflow the pie plate.) Bake for 1 hour and 10 minutes, until the apples are tender and juicy. Let cool for at least 10 minutes before serving warm. Top each slice with vanilla ice cream.

December

SHELBI'S SASSY SIXTEEN

Shelbi's Shrimp Egg Rolls

Mac and Cheese Cups

Creamed Collard Green Toasts

Ice Cream Cupcakes

HOLIDAY COCKTAIL PARTY

Hot Crab and Mushroom Dip with Toasted Pita Points

Smoked Cheesy Piggies in a Blanket

Sweet and Sour Mini-Meatballs

Blood Orange Bellinis

Chocolate Truffle Bites

CHRISTMAS DINNER

Neelys' Prime Rib with Ruby Port Sauce

Green Beans and Bacon

Maple-Glazed Carrots

Hearty Winter Greens Sauté

Smoky Scalloped Potatoes

Gina's Butterscotch Pudding Pots and Cashew Brittle

Shelbi's Sassy Sixteen

MAMA'S MEMORIES

GINA How do I even begin to process this? I still see Shelbi in her little onesie running around and "twirling" her pacifier. (I always told Pat, when a child starts doing tricks with her binky, she's too old for one!) She was the sweetest gift and bundle of joy, and still is. I've always felt, "She has been here before," because she did everything so fast—like walking at nine months. But that was probably because she had a bigger sister, and was always curious about what Spenser was doing. I remember how she would look with wonder at Spenser's legs as she walked. Shelbi was quick to learn and had such a big imagination. I embraced all of that until we started getting to another level, with "why this" and "why that" questions about the birds and the bees. Honey, it was too much! But, like I said, she was always inquisitive!

Once we got to fourteen, all I heard about was: "I can't wait until I turn sixteen." To which I thought, "I can!" When I was sassy sixteen, you couldn't tell me anything. . . .

But things today are so different: there's Facebook, MySpace, Twitter, texting, cyberbullying, and all kinds of craziness. So we really have to watch over our girls. Even though it may seem as though I'm always busy, I'm very involved in my daughters' lives, and being a mother is my most important job—before anything else. As mothers, we have to help our girls navigate and become their best selves. Some of this growing up is a bit harder for my girls, because their parents are on TV, but I respect the fact that Shelbi and Spenser don't think that they're any better than any of their friends—nor do they expect to be treated differently.

Shelbi always says, "People say I look like my daddy but I act like my mama." We have great conversations, and she is a shrimp- and collard-lover, just like me. As you can see from her menu below, she has a palate like a big girl. I can proudly say she's on her way to being a respectable, considerate, cordial, and conscientious young lady. (Yes, I know I am a little biased.) And so here we are, at sixteen: she's driving now and doing her thing, and I'm just trying to help her enhance her talents and gifts so that they can best serve her in the manner that she sees

fit. I think we have done a good job, because I see an amazing being on the way. Sixteen is just the beginning. . . . Look out, twenty-one!

DADDY'S MEMORIES

PAT Shelbi had her own way of arriving in this world. Gina called around 10:00 a.m. on November 30 and said, "I think it's time." So I jumped in my car and started the thirty-minute drive home. When I reached Gina, I figured out she was having pain every thirty to forty minutes. (I learned a little something in the Lamaze classes!) We got to the hospital, and they admitted her, but after we'd spent most of the day there, the doctors told us it was a false alarm—whew! On the way home, I needed to make a quick stop by the restaurant. I know what you're thinking: "Why in hell would you do that?" And it seemed easy, only a ten-minute errand. But when I got back to the car, the contractions had started again, so we headed straight back to the hospital. Arriving at the nurses' station, I told them, "Either admit her or me, because I'm not driving all the way home with her in this amount of pain." Shelbi Patrice Neely made her first appearance in the world at 12:15 a.m. on December 1. She had to make an entrance in her own time.

We were blessed to have Gina's godmother, whom we call "Nana," helping with Shelbi until she started preschool. Nana's known in our family as the "mother of all great cooks." She maintained a garden in her backyard, and prepared some of the most delicious meals I have *ever* eaten. Shelbi had the pleasure of being a part of Nana's kitchen just as Gina had been nearly thirty years ago, learning from the very same apron strings. When the girls were in school, we'd all gather in the kitchen at the end of the day, and the girls would do their homework at the kitchen table while Gina and I shared stories and cooked dinner. This was our time to communicate and connect as a family. Well, now Shelbi is a teenager, and, fortunately, she loves cooking, even after all that time in the kitchen! Cherish these years when your kids are young. Gina and I know too well that they will grow up, the house will become a little quieter, and the kids will have their own agendas, which might not always include you.

At sixteen, Shelbi excels in school, loves to read, and works at a nearby restaurant three to four days a week. (No, it's not Neely's. Gina and I always wanted our children to experience working for someone other than their parents, so that they might grow to appreciate what their parents really do!) I'm happy to say Shelbi is a lot like Spenser when it comes to birthday parties, and neither girl ever wanted one of those reality-TV sweet-sixteen parties where the parents spoil their kids with million-dollar events. Thank God we did not raise little divas or drama queens. We often remind our girls that when we were their age, big birthday celebrations were few and far between. Growing up in a house with five siblings and having other events and celebrations, it just wasn't feasible to have big parties on birthdays, too. But I'm very proud to celebrate Shelbi's Sassy Sixteen—although, I swear, it seems like it was just yesterday when I met my baby girl for the very first time.

SHELBI ON SIXTEEN

SHELBI For my Sassy Sixteen, we decorated the house in lime green, silver, hot pink, and black. There were goodie bags saying "Shelbi's Sassy at 16," filled up with hot-pink M&M's and mints that said "Sweet 16." It was a great night, with all my favorite foods and friends and family surrounding me.

From the time I was a little girl, I thought turning sixteen just meant being able to drive, but it means so much more. You're becoming a young adult in this very big world, and you have more responsibility. It's the next step in my life. Turning sixteen is embarking on that next journey into young adulthood, and I am ready to take it on!

Shelbi's Shrimp Egg Rolls

These egg rolls will have your teenager bragging on your behalf. Shrimp is Shelbi's favorite, and she always loved egg rolls, so she thought this stuffing combo was a perfect match. You can prep the rolls early, or even the night before, so all you need to do before the guests arrive is drop them in the fryer. **MAKES 12 EGG ROLLS**

2 tablespoons soy sauce

2 teaspoons roasted sesame oil

1 teaspoon sugar

1 teaspoon crushed red-pepper flakes

2 tablespoons vegetable oil

1-inch piece of fresh ginger root, peeled and grated

3 cloves garlic, finely chopped

4 green onions, finely chopped

1 carrot, peeled and grated

½ head Napa cabbage, thinly sliced

¾ pound large shrimp, peeled and deveined, tails removed, chopped

12 egg-roll wrappers (found in refrigerated section of grocery store)

1 egg, beaten

Peanut oil, for frying

Sweet and sour sauce, for dipping (store-bought)

Whisk together the soy sauce, sesame oil, sugar, and red-pepper flakes in a small bowl, and set aside.

Heat the vegetable oil in a large skillet over medium-high heat. Toss in the ginger, garlic, and green onions, and sauté for 1 minute, until fragrant. Stir in the carrot and cabbage, and continue to stir until the vegetables have softened, another 4 minutes. Push the vegetables to the outer edges of the skillet, and add the shrimp to the center of the pan. Cook for another 3 minutes, then stir the vegetables and shrimp together and add the soy-sauce mixture. Let cool completely.

Set a wrapper on your work surface with a corner directed toward you, and brush the edges of the egg-roll wrapper with the beaten egg. Place ¼ cup of the shrimp mixture on the lower third of each wrapper. Fold the bottom corner portion of the wrapper up over the filling. Fold both the side corners inward, and roll the wrapper up like a burrito. Repeat with the remaining wrappers.

Heat 4 inches of peanut oil in a large, heavy-bottomed saucepan until it reaches 350 degrees F. (For tips on deep-frying, see page 19.)

Add the egg rolls, in batches of four or five, to the hot oil, and cook until they are crisp and golden brown, about 3 to 5 minutes. Remove them from the oil, and let drain on a paper-towel-lined sheet tray. Serve with sweet and sour sauce.

Mac and Cheese Cups

If there is a comfort food for teens, it's mac and cheese. Spenser and Shelbi absolutely love it! These little mac-and-cheese cups are both fun to make and great to eat. Adding panko bread crumbs creates a nice crunch that will satisfy adults as well. **MAKES 12 CUPS**

8 ounces elbow macaroni

Kosher salt and freshly ground black pepper

3 tablespoons butter, plus more for greasing

1 small shallot, finely chopped

2 tablespoons all-purpose flour

2 cups whole milk, warm

1 teaspoon Dijon mustard

2 cups shredded cheddar cheese

½ cup panko bread crumbs

Preheat the oven to 350 degrees F. Butter a twelve-cup muffin tin.

Cook the pasta in a large pot of boiling salted water until al dente, then drain in a colander.

Melt the butter in a large saucepan. Add the shallot, and sauté until tender, about 3 minutes. Add the flour, and stir until it thickens and reaches a golden-blond color, about 2 minutes. Slowly whisk in the warm milk, bringing up to a simmer, and stir until it thickens. Stir in mustard, and season with salt and pepper. Let the sauce simmer on low heat for 5 minutes, until thick enough to coat the back of a spoon. Stir in the cheese a handful at a time, then stir in the cooked macaroni.

Divide the macaroni among the cups in the muffin tin, and sprinkle with bread crumbs. Bake for 15 minutes, or until they're nicely golden brown on top. Let them rest for 5 minutes, then slide a knife around the edges to remove from the muffin tin, and serve.

Creamed Collard Green Toasts

SHELBI One of my fondest memories is of Mom cooking collard greens on Saturday afternoon in preparation for dinner after church on Sunday. It was like a mini-Thanksgiving feast!

GINA It's true, Shelbi grew up on collards, and she got that love from me. Nana's garden had rows and rows of those big leafy plants. Sautéing these Southern favorites in a buttery onion-and-garlic sauce is the best, and putting them on toast is just another twist to stay creative with collards. **SERVES 8 TO 10**

Kosher salt

1 large bunch collard greens, washed well

3 tablespoons butter

1 shallot, finely chopped

3 cloves garlic, finely chopped

1½ cups heavy cream

¼ cup grated Parmesan cheese

Freshly ground black pepper

¼ cup extra-virgin olive oil

¼ teaspoon crushed red-pepper flakes

1 baguette, cut into ½-inch slices

Preheat the oven to 375 degrees F, and arrange racks in the middle. Bring a large pot of salted water to a boil.

Remove the stems and center ribs from the collard greens. Stack about six leaves on top of each other, roll into a cigar shape, and slice into thin ribbons. Add the collard greens by handfuls to the boiling water, and cook until tender, about 15 minutes. Drain well in a colander.

Melt the butter in a large skillet until it foams. Once it's foaming, toss in the shallot and garlic and cook over moderate heat until they have softened, about 6 minutes. Stir in the cream, and simmer, stirring occasionally, until reduced by half, about 15 minutes. Add the greens to the cream, and toss until warmed through, about 3 minutes. Stir in the Parmesan cheese, and add salt and pepper to taste. Keep warm.

While the cream is reducing, mix the olive oil, red-pepper flakes, salt, and pepper in a small ramekin. Brush the bread slices on both sides with the olive oil. Place the bread on two sheet trays, and toast until golden and crisp, about 15 minutes. Set aside.

Place the toasted bread on a platter, and top with spoonfuls of the creamed collards. Serve hot or at room temperature.

Ice Cream Cupcakes

SHELBI I love ice cream, anything ice cream! (I guess I'm a lot like Dad.) But I also love icing and cake, so I thought it would be a great idea to mix ice cream and a cupcake, and make a mini–ice cream cake. That way, everyone can have their cake and ice cream, too.

GINA AND PAT These make us want to be a teenager again, too. Luckily, that's not a requirement for making or eating them. Just check out the ingredients and you know you're in for a real treat. Make a dozen, no matter how small your party is, because they'll keep in the freezer for several days. **MAKES 12 CUPCAKES**

12 Oreo cookies, finely crushed

3 tablespoons melted butter

2 pints Rocky Road ice cream, softened

½ cup caramel ice cream topping

1½ cups whipped topping, thawed

¼ cup rainbow sprinkles

12 Maraschino cherries

Line a twelve-cup muffin tin with decorative liners.

Combine the crushed cookie pieces and butter in a large bowl. Divide the cookie mixture among the twelve cupcake liners, and press down to form a crust. Add a large scoop of ice cream to each cupcake, and carefully spread to cover the crust and fill the cup. Drizzle each cupcake with caramel, and then pipe the whipped topping on the cupcakes, using a pastry bag fitted with a large star tip. Top each cupcake with sprinkles and a cherry. Freeze for 3 hours, or until firm.

Holiday Cocktail Party

PAT Come October, friends and family start asking, "Are you doing a Thanksgiving, Christmas, or New Year's Eve party?" I don't know if they keep coming back for the food, the music, the fellowship, or to see what new dances Gina has learned, but most of them know they are going to get all of the above. Over the years, the menu has continued to grow, as have the guest list (fifty to seventy people) and the entertainment. I can normally be found in a corner, just watching in amazement.

Our schedule these days is as busy as a one-eyed dog in a meat market, so we can't plan and prepare for holiday parties like we used to. But, thank God, for some reason we still have this wonderful tradition. In the last couple of years, however, we've changed the way we celebrate: instead of hosting the three holiday parties, Gina and I now host one big one: *the* Holiday Party. This one feels even more special than its predecessors, and maybe it's because we don't get a chance to spend as much time with our loved ones as we used to.

So, if your schedule has become as hectic as ours, maybe you should try throwing one big celebration. Don't forget the music and dancing! The dishes on this menu will create a memorable evening for all and will have your family and friends telling you not to forget them next year.

GINA What could be better than piling all the holiday cheer into one great evening? I like to pull out the "master" pig-shaped barbecue, with the platter on her back, and add a big bow around her neck. She sits center-stage, holding the Bellinis, as if she is saying, "Take one, we all need a little spirit." You guys know I talk to my piggies, and they talk back. Thank goodness, or somebody would think I was cuckoo around here. . . . Happy holidays!

Hot Crab and Mushroom Dip with Toasted Pita Points

GINA Set out a unique dip to get this cheer rolling in! No one ever really expects you to go to the trouble of making something as special as a warm crab dip—but they sure are happy if you do. It adds a festive, caring quality to the party in the same way a great piece of jewelry can make a whole outfit special. **SERVES 4 TO 6**

4 tablespoons butter

1 shallot, finely chopped

3 cloves garlic, finely chopped

½ pound button mushrooms, roughly chopped

¼ cup all-purpose flour

2 cups half-and-half

¼ cup dry white wine

¼ cup finely grated Parmesan cheese

1 cup shredded Fontina cheese

12 ounces lump crabmeat, picked through for shells or cartilage

2 tablespoons chopped fresh parsley

Dash of hot sauce, preferably Tabasco

Dash of Worcestershire sauce

Kosher salt and freshly ground black pepper

Preheat the oven to 425 degrees F.

Melt the butter in a medium saucepan over medium-high heat. Add the shallot, garlic, and mushrooms, and sauté, stirring frequently, until the liquid cooks off and they become tender, about 3 minutes. Stir in the flour, and cook for 1 minute more, until the flour reaches a light-blond color. Slowly whisk in the half-and-half, and stir until the sauce thickens.

Pour the wine into the saucepan, and stir in the Parmesan and Fontina by handfuls until the cheese has melted. Fold in the crab and parsley; season with the hot sauce and Worcestershire. Add salt and pepper to taste.

Spoon the mixture into a 1½-quart casserole dish. Bake for 15 minutes, until bubbly and golden brown. Serve with toasted pita points (recipe follows).

TOASTED PITA POINTS

SERVES 4 TO 6

Five 6-inch pitas

3 tablespoons olive oil

Kosher salt and freshly ground black pepper

Preheat the oven to 375 degrees F.

Brush the pitas lightly with olive oil, then cut each pita into eight wedges. Arrange the pita on two sheet trays, sprinkle with salt and pepper, and bake for 5 to 7 minutes, until crisp.

Smoked Cheesy Piggies in a Blanket

GINA It wouldn't be my party without some piggies, and these are the good old-fashioned finger-food kind. Our twist is to serve them with barbecue sauce. Watch your guests come runnin'—they'll be shamelessly stuffin' 'em down!

MAKES 48 BITES

Two 8-ounce cans prepared crescent dough

¼ cup Neely's BBQ sauce (see page 37), plus more for serving

¼ cup shredded cheddar cheese

48 smoked cocktail wieners

Butter, for greasing

2 eggs, lightly beaten

3 tablespoons raw sesame seeds

Preheat the oven to 350 degrees F.

Cut each triangle of crescent-roll dough into thirds lengthwise, making three small strips from each roll.

Brush the dough strips lightly with BBQ sauce, and sprinkle with cheese. Place a cocktail wiener on the wider end of each piece of dough, and roll up.

Place the piggies, seam side down, on a greased sheet tray. Brush with the beaten eggs and sprinkle with sesame seeds. Bake for 12 to 15 minutes, or until golden brown. Serve while warm with extra BBQ sauce for dipping.

Neelys' Prime Rib with Ruby Port Sauce

GINA Outside of England, I know it may seem out of the ordinary to have prime rib, but after having so much ham or turkey, we like to mix it up a little bit—and Pat loves a juicy steak. That's one thing that's nice about the Neely household: you can expect the unexpected. I remember, the first time we served it, everybody was shocked and talked about how it looked so pretty, they didn't want to slice into it. But if you know my brother Ronnie and Pat's brother Mark, that thought about not slicing the roast didn't last very long. And tasting this ruby port sauce is almost as fabulous as opening that present you've been hinting at all season. **SERVES 6 TO 8**

4 cloves garlic, smashed and peeled

2 tablespoons kosher salt

2 tablespoons finely chopped fresh rosemary

2 to 3 tablespoons olive oil

2 teaspoons freshly ground black pepper

¼ teaspoon crushed red-pepper flakes

One 8-pound bone-in prime-rib roast (3 or 4 ribs)

Mash the garlic and salt with a mortar and pestle until a paste is formed. Add the rosemary, and smash all together. Scrape the paste into a small bowl along with the olive oil, black pepper, and crushed red pepper.

Spread the herb-and-garlic paste all over the meat. Cover with plastic wrap, and place in the fridge to marinate for at least 8 hours. Allow the meat to come to room temperature for 1 to 2 hours before roasting. (This will ensure even cooking.)

Preheat your oven to 450 degrees F. Adjust a rack to the middle of the oven.

Remove the plastic wrap, and place the meat in a large roasting pan. Roast for 20 minutes, then reduce the oven temperature to 350 degrees, and continue to cook until a thermometer inserted into the thickest part of the roast without touching the bone reads 125 degrees for medium rare, or continue to cook until it reaches 130 to 135 for medium, about 2 hours and 20 minutes more.

Remove the roast from the oven, tent with foil, and let rest for 20 minutes before carving.

Serve with the ruby port sauce (recipe follows).

NOTE Get the rib rubbed with the spices the day before, and set aside in the fridge.

RUBY PORT SAUCE

MAKES 2 CUPS

3 tablespoons butter, divided

2 shallots, finely chopped

2 cloves garlic, minced

1¼ cups ruby port

4 cups beef stock, homemade or low-sodium

Kosher salt and freshly ground black pepper

Melt 2 tablespoons of the butter in a medium saucepan set over medium heat. Once the butter foams, toss in the shallots and garlic, and sauté until soft and tender, about 3 or 4 minutes. Pour the port and beef stock into the saucepan, and bring to a simmer. Let reduce for about 20 minutes, or until you have about 2 cups of brothlike sauce. Whisk in the remaining tablespoon of butter for a touch of added thickness and gloss. Season to taste with salt and pepper.

Green Beans and Bacon

Our girls are huge lovers of green beans, so they are a must-have on the menu. (We try to accommodate everyone in some way or another.) Of course, the smokiness of the pig doesn't hurt, either. **SERVES 6 TO 8**

2½ pounds green beans, trimmed

Kosher salt and freshly ground black pepper

½ pound bacon slices, roughly chopped

1 small yellow onion, finely chopped

3 cloves garlic, minced

1 teaspoon crushed red-pepper flakes

½ cup chopped pecans, toasted

Juice of ½ lemon

Toss the green beans into a large pot of boiling salted water and cook until bright green in color and tender-crisp, about 5 minutes. Drain the beans, and shock them in a large bowl of ice water to stop the cooking. Drain the beans again, and pat dry.

Cook the bacon in a large, heavy sauté pan until crisp, about 5 minutes. Remove the bacon to a paper-towel-lined plate to drain. Spoon off the excess grease, leaving 2 tablespoons in the pan. Add the onion to the pan, and sauté until soft and very tender, about 4 or 5 minutes. Sprinkle in the garlic and red-pepper flakes, and sauté until just fragrant, about 1 more minute. Add the reserved green beans and the pecans, and cook until heated through, about 5 or 6 minutes more. Return the bacon to the pan, pour in the lemon juice, and toss. Season to taste with salt and pepper. Remove to a serving bowl.

Maple-Glazed Carrots

PAT We all love carrots in this household, but no one more than Gina. Adding the maple syrup brings out their natural sweetness, giving some sugar for my sugar. (Maybe she'll let me steal some back later on!) **SERVES 8**

2 tablespoons butter

1 tablespoon olive oil

2½ pounds carrots, peeled, halved if thick, trimmed into 1-inch pieces

Kosher salt and freshly ground black pepper

1 cup chicken broth

¼ cup real maple syrup

Juice of ½ lemon

2 tablespoons finely chopped fresh parsley

Heat the butter and olive oil in a large, heavy-bottomed saucepan over medium-high heat. Once the butter foams, sauté the carrots until they are crisp-tender, about 4 or 5 minutes. Season with salt and pepper. Pour the broth and maple syrup into the pan. Cover, reduce heat to medium, and simmer for 10 minutes.

Remove cover, and continue to cook for another 6 to 8 minutes over high heat, until the carrots are tender and glazed with the syrup. Toss with the lemon juice and parsley, and serve.

Hearty Winter Greens Sauté

This dish is the king of all veggies. Turnip greens, kale, Swiss chard, and mustard greens all join forces in a hearty, healthy side dish. Putting them all together may go against your style, but, trust us, the combo is surprisingly delicious. (Just ask the girls; they were skeptical at first, too.) As you know, we can all use more veggies!

SERVES 6 TO 8

1 bunch mustard greens, cleaned

1 bunch turnip greens, cleaned

1 bunch kale, cleaned

1 bunch Swiss chard, cleaned

2 tablespoons olive oil

1 large yellow onion, thinly sliced

4 cloves garlic, thinly sliced

Kosher salt and freshly ground
    black pepper

1½ cups chicken broth

Juice of 1 lemon

Remove the center stems from the cleaned greens, and slice the leaves into ½-inch ribbons.

Pour the oil into a large Dutch oven over medium-high heat. Once it's hot, add the onion and garlic, and sauté until tender and fragrant, about 4 minutes. Season with salt and pepper.

Stir in the ribbons of mustard and turnip greens and kale in batches, adding the next batch as the one prior wilts down. Once all the greens are added to the pot, pour in the broth and cook for 10 minutes. Then add the ribbons of Swiss chard, and cover with a lid. Let simmer for 5 more minutes. Taste for seasoning, and add the lemon juice. Spoon the vegetables into a large serving bowl.

Smoky Scalloped Potatoes

Sometimes the best gift in the world on Christmas is to serve your children one of their favorite dishes. And, boy oh boy, does Spenser love cheesy potatoes! Warning: this recipe is extremely addictive. We use smoked paprika to add a hearty smokiness that's like nothing else out there. **SERVES 6**

4 tablespoons butter, divided

1 small shallot, finely chopped

4 garlic cloves, minced

Salt and freshly ground black pepper to taste

3 cups half-and-half

2 teaspoons smoked paprika

2½ pounds russet potatoes, peeled, thinly sliced

1 cup grated sharp white cheddar cheese

⅓ cup freshly grated Parmesan cheese

Preheat the oven to 400 degrees F.

Butter a 13-by-9-inch casserole dish with 2 tablespoons butter.

Melt the remaining 2 tablespoons butter in a large saucepan over medium heat. Once the butter foams, add the shallot and garlic, and sauté until softened, about 3 to 4 minutes. Season with salt and pepper, and pour in the half-and-half, smoked paprika, and potatoes. Bring to a low simmer. Allow to cook for 5 minutes.

Pour half of the potato mixture into the buttered casserole dish. Shake the pan to arrange the potatoes in a single layer. Sprinkle half of each of the cheeses on top of the bottom layer. Add the remaining potatoes, and shake again to arrange in a layer. Sprinkle on the remaining cheese, cover with foil, and bake for 45 minutes, or until bubbling. Remove the foil, and place back in the oven for 15 minutes more, or until the potatoes and cheese are golden and browned.

Let stand 15 minutes before serving.

CASHEW BRITTLE

½ cup corn syrup

1½ cups granulated white sugar

½ teaspoon table salt

½ teaspoon baking soda

1 cup raw unsalted cashews

2 tablespoons butter

Line a nonstick sheet pan with parchment or a silicone mat, and set aside.

Heat the corn syrup, sugar, and salt in a medium saucepan set over medium-high heat. Cook until the temperature reaches 310 degrees F on a candy thermometer. Once the mixture reaches 310 degrees F, remove from the stove; quickly add the baking soda, cashews, and butter, and keep stirring constantly. The mixture will stay opaque.

Carefully pour the hot mixture onto the mat- or parchment-covered sheet pan, and spread across the pan with wooden spoon. Cool for 1½ hours. Break into 2-inch pieces.

NOTE A silicone mat works best to avoid a sticky clean-up; do not use waxed paper, which will melt and stick under the heat of the candy.

Recipes by Course

APPETIZERS AND SMALL BITES

All-Nighter Trail Mix
Ancho-Spiced Nuts
Bourbon BBQ Glazed Ribs
Chicken Pot Stickers
Country-Fried Jalapeño Poppers
Crab-Stuffed Mushroom Caps
Creamed Collard Green Toasts
Devils on Horseback
Drunken Goat Cheese and
    Tomato Mini-Sandwiches
Fresh Mango Salsa and
    Homemade Tortilla Chips
Gina's "Double Pig" Grilled Potato Skins
Grilled Mini-Pizzas
Grilled Shrimp and Pineapple Skewers
Grilled Bacon-Wrapped Shrimp
Homemade BBQ Potato Chips
Memphis-Style Popcorn
Mile-High Memphis BBQ Nachos
New Orleans BBQ Shrimp
Pat's Sweet and Spicy Grilled Wings
Shelbi's Shrimp Egg Rolls
Simple Deviled Eggs
Smoked Cheesy Piggies in a Blanket
Smokin' Snack Mix
Spicy Grilled Cheese Bread
Spicy Grilled Shrimp Cocktail
Sweet and Sour Mini-Meatballs

DIPS, SAUCES, AND RUBS

Seven-Layer Dip
Buttermilk Dressing
Chipotle Cocktail Sauce
Chipotle Mayo
Comeback Sauce
Cranberry Chipotle Relish
Game-Day Glaze
Homemade Bourbon-Caramel-Pecan Sauce
Hot Crab and Mushroom Dip
    with Toasted Pita Points
Just-Right Dry Rub for Steaks
Mint Vinaigrette

Neely's Barbecue Rub
Neely's BBQ Sauce
Roasted Red Pepper Feta Dressing
Smoky Blue Cheese Dipping Sauce
Sweet and Spicy Orange Dipping Sauce
Sweet Cherry-Cola BBQ Sauce
Sweet-Pickle Mayo
Sun-Dried-Tomato Mayo
Tanya's Spicy Spinach Dip

SOUPS AND STEWS

Beer-Braised Brisket Chili
Gina's Hoppin' John Soup
Pumpkin and Sweet Potato Bisque

SALADS

Big Green Salad with Cherry Tomatoes and
    Buttermilk Dressing
Classic Picnic Potato Salad
Crunchy Slaw
German Potato Salad
Green Herb Salad with
    Roasted Red Pepper Feta Dressing
Marinated Broccoli Salad
Mustard Slaw
Neely's Coleslaw
Roasted Tomato and Asparagus Salad
Smoky Corn and Zucchini Salad
Summer Rice Salad

BREADS AND BISCUITS

Angel Biscuits
Corn Bread Sticks
Hush Puppies

SANDWICHES, BURGERS, AND PIZZAS

Deluxe BBQ Burgers
Fig and Arugula Flatbread
Gina's Favorite Chicken and Spinach Pizza
Grilled Smoked Sausage and Pepper Sandwich
One-Handed Turkey Burgers
Southern-Style Fish Tacos
Spenser's Fried Chicken Sliders

PASTAS AND CASSEROLES

BBQ Chili Mac
Chicken and Biscuits

Green Pasta Salad
Mac and Cheese Cups
Sexy Seafood Pasta

ENTRÉES

Char-Grilled Rib Eye with
    Roasted Shallot and Herb Butter
Easy If-Ya-Ain't-Got-a-Smoker BBQ Pork
Fried Catfish
Game-Day Grilled Turkey Drumsticks
Grilled Lobsters with
    Lemon Basil Butter
Honey BBQ Sticky Drumsticks
Memphis Fried Turkey
Neelys' If-You've-Got-a-Smoker BBQ Pork
Neelys' Prime Rib with Ruby Port Sauce
Pat's Deep-Fried Cornish Game Hens
Pat's Grilled Leg of Lamb with Mint Vinaigrette
Pat's Smoked Chicken
Smothered Pork Chops
Sweet Cola BBQ Beef Ribs

SIDE DISHES

The Best Mashed Potatoes
Buttered and Spiced Spring Peas
Corn Bread and Collard Dressing
Dirty-Rice Collard Green Bundles
Green Beans and Bacon
Grilled Potato Wedges
Hearty Winter Greens Sauté
Mama Neely's Baked Beans
Maple-Glazed Carrots
Onion Rings
Roasted Broccoli with Garlic and
    Cherry Tomatoes
Roasted Corn on a Stick
Roasted Red Potatoes
Sautéed Kale with Garlic
Smashed Fingerling Potatoes
Smoky Grilled Corn with Zesty Lime Butter
Smoky Scalloped Potatoes
Whipped Garlicky Mashed Potatoes

DESSERTS

Apple Crumb Pie
Banana Cake with Coconut Frosting

Blueberry Pie
Bourbon Bread Pudding
Chewy Pecan Bars
Chocolate and Peanut Butter Brownie Bites
Chocolate Tartlets
Chocolate Truffle Bites
Creamsicle Float
Devil's Food Cake
Easy Ice Cream Sandwiches
Fresh Strawberry Ice Cream with Shortbread
    Crumble
Gina's Butterscotch Pudding Pots and Cashew
    Brittle
Grilled Apricot and Peach Shortcake
Ice Cream Cupcakes
Ice Cream Sundaes with Homemade Bourbon-
    Caramel-Pecan Sauce
Lemon Squares
Pat's Quarterback Cookies
Poached Peaches and Cream
Shot of Love

BREAKFAST

Blue Ribbon Blueberry Muffins
Delightful Asparagus Frittata
Homemade Turkey Sausage Patties
Rise and Shine Granola
Smoky Sweet Potato Cakes with
    Mama Callie's Maple Syrup

DRINKS AND LIBATIONS

Berry Sangria
Blackberry Mojitos
Blood Orange Bellinis
Flower Power
Frozen Mango Margaritas
Frozen Memphis Mint Juleps
Gina's Gin Cooler
Love Potion #9
Mama's Day Off Cocktail
Michelada Beer Cocktails
Minted Iced Tea
Peach Spritzer
Sparkling Raspberry Lemonade
Watermelon Cooler

Acknowledgments

PAT Gina, you have truly made my life WHOLE! You have supported me, loved me, and been the best partner a man could ask for. And to my entire family, thank you for your lifelong support.

GINA Thank you to my friend, partner, and husband, my diva daughters and my family; may all our different traditions live on within you. Thank you to my mother for showing me the way and always being there for me, and thanks to my two B's (Belinda and Brenda).

PAT AND GINA We'd like to thank the Neely team: if we were in the business of football, we would have several Super Bowl rings by now. To Jonathan Russo at Artists Agency; Janis Donnaud, our literary agent; and to Paul Bogaards and the Knopf team—without you, we would not have been able to share these wonderful stories with the entire world.

Many thanks to Brianna Beaudry and Ann Volkwein: y'all know you are our "girls"! Without your commitment, hard work, and fantastic dedication, these delicious dishes would not express the love that we share. And thanks to Ben Fink for visually bringing our story to life.

And finally, to every fan of *Down Home with the Neelys* who has been with us since day one, may we always encourage and enlighten your spirit and share the greatest gift of all LAUGHTER AND TOGETHERNESS! Thank you for showing the LOVE and enjoying our stories of memorable celebrations and the dishes we are so proud of.

Now GO THROW A PARTY!

A NOTE ABOUT THE AUTHORS

As co-owners of Neely's Bar-B-Que, Pat and Gina Neely have turned their family restaurant into one of the most successful barbecue restaurants in the South, with locations in Memphis and Nashville. They share the secrets behind their favorite dishes and their passion for food, family, and fun on the Food Network's hit *Down Home with the Neelys*. Their debut cookbook of the same name was a *New York Times* best seller, and they recently opened their first New York City restaurant, Neely's Barbecue Parlor.

High school sweethearts in the 1980s, Pat and Gina live with their daughters, Spenser and Shelbi, in Memphis where they enjoy cooking at home with family and friends.

Ann Volkwein is a *New York Times* best-selling food and lifestyle author based in New York City and Austin, Texas. Her previous books include *The Arthur Avenue Cookbook*, *Chinatown New York*, *Mixt Greens* (with Andrew Swallow), and, with Guy Fieri, *Diners, Drive-Ins, and Dives*; *More Diners Drive-Ins, and Dives*; and *Guy Fieri Food*.

A NOTE ON THE TYPE

This book was set in Chaparral, an Adobe original typeface designed by Carol Twombly and released in 1997. The inspiration for Chaparral was a page of lettering from a sixteenth-century manuscript, adapted by Twombly into a readable slab serif design. Unlike geometric slab serif fonts, Chaparral has varying letter proportions that give it an accessible and friendly appearance. Chaparral was the last typeface Twombly designed before she left Adobe and perhaps retired from type design in 1999.

COMPOSED BY NORTH MARKET STREET GRAPHICS, LANCASTER, PENNSYLVANIA

PRINTED AND BOUND BY RR DONNELLEY, CRAWFORDSVILLE, INDIANA

DESIGNED BY MAGGIE HINDERS